Francesco Filippi is a historian of mentalities and an educator who has specialized in the relationship between memory and the present. He is co-founder of Deina, an association that organises trips of memory and training courses all over Italy. Filippi is the author of five books including the Italian bestseller *Mussolini Also Did A Lot of Good* (Baraka Books 2021). He lives in Trento, Italy.

Domenic Cusmano is a Montreal communications professional, photojournalist, and translator whose previous translations include books from Italian and French into English. Publisher and editor of *Accenti Magazine*, he holds degrees from the Université de Montréal and McGill University. His work as a photojournalist has taken him throughout Europe, Africa, and South America.

Robin Philpot is publisher of Baraka Books and author of seven books in French and English including *Rwanda and the New Scramble for Africa*. He lives in Montreal.

T0244302

BUT WE BUILT ROADS FOR THEM

Francesco Filippi

BUT WE BUILT ROADS FOR THEM

The Lies, Racism, and Amnesia that Bury Italy's Colonial Past

Translated by
Domenic Cusmano

Baraka
Books

Montréal

Original title: *Noi Pero Gli Abbiamo Fatto Les Strade, Le colonie italiane tra bugie, razzismi et amnesie.*
Francesco Filippi, Bollati Boringhieri Editore, ©2021

ISBN 978-1-77186-341-4 pbk; 978-1-77186-353-7 epub; 978-1-77186-354-4 pdf

Cover and book design by Folio infographie
Foreword by Robin Philpot
Translation by Domenic Cusmano
Cover photo: Italian troops in Libya, 1911
Editing and proofreading: Robin Philpot, Anne Marie Marko

Legal Deposit, 2nd quarter 2024
Bibliothèque et Archives nationales du Québec
Library and Archives Canada

Published by Baraka Books of Montreal

Printed and bound in Quebec
Trade Distribution & Returns
Canada – UTP Distribution: UTPdistribution.com
United States
Independent Publishers Group: IPGbook.com

We acknowledge the support from the Société de développement des entreprises culturelles (SODEC) and the Government of Quebec tax credit for book publishing administered by SODEC.

CONTENTS

To Efrem and Raffaele,
For the past,
but especially for the future.

Filippi's Template for Canada and Other Countries

"We also have no history of colonialism... So we have all of the things that many people admire about the great powers but none of the things that threaten or bother them."

Stephen Harper, Pittsburgh G20 meeting, 2009

When former Prime Minister Harper declared at the September 2009 G20 meeting in Pittsburgh that "We also have no history of colonialism," he was simply echoing the words and thoughts of many of his predecessors and a large portion of the Canadian population. Fortunately, he was criticized – though not widely enough. Most criticism rightly targeted Canada's ignoble history of colonization of lands belonging to First Nations and the crimes that ensued.

Serious scrutiny of Canada's colonial past, however, would require that we look at Canada's role internationally. That we turn over the stones carefully and selectively placed to erase a past that, if remembered, might run counter to the identity that Canada's current leaders are trying to adopt. At the same time, it could thwart the roll-out Canada's foreign policy in the 2020s.

With the world inching closer to wide-scale war and Canada coming into conflict with countries on all continents, such an examination should be a priority. Understanding our colonial past will help understand, and perhaps avoid, future international conflict.

Francesco Filippi, by challenging the accepted narrative about Italy's colonial past, has provided an excellent template for Canada and other countries. He shows how collective memory takes shape and how it sweeps vast swaths of history under the rug. Perhaps more importantly, he shows how that collective memory becomes an obstacle to solving today's crises, both internationally and on the domestic scene.

So how would that apply to Canada?

As an extension of the British empire from 1763 until the Act of Westminster of 1931, British North America, renamed Canada in 1867, played a crucial and active role in Britain's imperial expansion. Canada had no foreign policy. Everything was decided in London and announced to Canadians, who more often than not willingly joined in. (Among the notable exceptions was French Canada's opposition to participation in imperial wars.) The slave trade was at its peak at the beginning of those 168 years, and by the end, the British empire had expanded on all continents to a point where the sun never set.

Some will say that little of that history belongs to Canadians today. However, evidence to the contrary 'lies across Canada,' to paraphrase James Loewen's book *Lies Across America*. The toponymy, monuments, and holidays leave little doubt about where Canada stood in those imperial conquests. The following examples are just the tip of an iceberg.

Following the discovery in 2021 of the graves of more than 1000 indigenous children around three residential schools, First Nations of Manitoba toppled the monument to Queen Victoria in front of the Manitoba Legislature. Their action rang bells around the world because of what the British empire had inflicted upon peoples worldwide in Victoria's name.

Yet Victoria is probably the most celebrated person in Canada. Monuments or streets honour her in almost every city. Each year on May 24, Canadians celebrate "Victoria Day." To be precise, Canadians do but Quebecers do not. In 2022, Victoria Day (Fête de la Reine) was abolished and replaced by the Fête nationale des Patriotes in memory of the Patriote rebellions against British domination in 1837-38 and the hanging of their leaders—by Queen Victoria's colonial government.

When Louis Riel led a provisional government in 1870, which resulted in the creation of the Province of Manitoba, British Troops led by Marshal Garnet Wolseley were sent to crush the rebellion. Wolseley was not some run-of-the-mill British officer. In fact, he became a symbol of the planetary expansion of the British Empire in the 19th century, being named Viscount in 1885 by Queen Victoria. Before putting down Riel's Red River resistance, Wolseley had earned his colours in the colonial repression in India in 1857, also known as India's first war of independence. He was then sent to China in 1860 where he commanded the troops that destroyed the Old Summer Palace in Beijing, a "wonder of the world," according to Victor Hugo.

After Riel, as Governor of the Gold Coast (now Ghana), Wolseley headed the British troops that took Kumase, capital city of the Ashanti Kingdom, which he razed. He also led British troops to put down anti-colonial rebellions in Egypt, in Khartoum, and in South Africa. Despite this violent colonial history, Canada still honours Wolseley. A town in Saskatchewan is called Wolseley while streets in Montreal, Toronto, Thunder Bay, and Winnipeg bear his name.

After Victoria, Lord Elgin or James Bruce, 8th Earl of Elgin, is among the most celebrated people in Canada. Elgin was Governor General of Canada from 1847 to 1854. Elgin Street, a stone's throw from the Canadian Parliament in Ottawa, is among the most important thoroughfares in the

Canadian capital. Government offices including the Canada Council of the Arts have an Elgin Street address. Bruce Peninsula is also named after him as are streets and parks across the country.

Do Canadians realize that Elgin is despised in China and disliked in India? As British High Commissioner and Plenipotentiary in China, he led the British bombing campaign of Guangzhou (Canton) in 1858. In Beijing, Elgin personally ordered the destruction and the looting of the Summer Palace in 1860. Elgin then became Viceroy of India.

Neither China nor India have forgotten Lord Elgin. Were Canada to acknowledge this past and take corrective action, both China and India would likely interpret it as a significant gesture in favour of improved diplomatic and trade relations.

Baraka Books is proud to publish Francesco Filippi's *But We Built Roads for Them*. Hopefully it will inspire a writer in Canada to take on the challenge of showing how Canada's collective memory has been shaped and blotted out Canada's colonial history. Here is a possible title:

BUT WE HAVE NO HISTORY OF COLONIALISM
The Lies, Racism and Amnesia
that Bury Canada's Colonial Past

Robin Philpot, Publisher

Introduction

Some Parts Went Missing

Pieces of history, pieces of division
Pieces of Resistance, pieces of nation
Pieces of House of Savoy, pieces of Bourbons
Pieces of rope, pieces of soap
Pieces of stick, pieces of carrot
Pieces of engine against pieces of wheel
Pieces of hunger, pieces of immigration
Pieces of tears, pieces of people
Everyone is a child of his defeat
Everyone is free with his fate
Throw away the key and go to Africa, Celestino!

Francesco De Gregori,
"Go to Africa, Celestino!" (song, 2005)

In the twentieth century, Italy experienced a series of major upheavals on the path to building what we will call "a collective memory,"[1] that is, the construct of historical facts that we consider part of our society's heritage.

The way of remembering what is intended as a common past underwent many abrupt changes of direction in a relatively short period of time. Generations of Italians saw many different narratives pass before their eyes: the value system of a nascent unified Italy; the different "battles of memory" put forth alternately by the Fascist regime, the Resistance, and the democratic reorganizers of the country; and the accounts emanating from the political and social upheavals of the mid-1990s. After many acrimonious debates over the many fractures of the past, the result is a reshuffling and revision of the major themes of Italian history.[2]

During these ongoing machinations, all aspects of the past have been discussed, rehashed and reconstructed time and again. Countless texts have been written, dramatizations filmed, and social media channels created—on the Unification of Italy, on the Fascist massacres, on the discovery of America, on Dante, on the upheavals of 1968—all dedicated to the many ways of revising, refreshing, and re-analysing events that are indisputably part of our common past. All of our country's "important" moments have been read and re-read over time.

Actually, no; almost all of them. There is one aspect of Italian history, in the period in question, that has not substantially been part of the public discourse with the aim of fostering a new interpretation, bringing about a new collective awareness, or even just making it a rhetorical weapon of daily political debate. We are talking about Italian colonialism.

This was a historically long and complex period. It began with the creation of the first Italian colonial outpost in 1882, when the government of prime minister Agostino Depretis acquired the rights to administer an area in Assab Bay on the Red Sea;[3] it ended when the Italian flag was lowered for the last time on African soil in Mogadishu, Somalia, on July 1, 1960.[4]

Lasting nearly eighty years, Italian colonialism can be regarded as one of the most substantial undertakings, both in terms of existence and continuity, in Italy's troubled history. It has had obvious repercussions on the country's history, politics, and society. Yet, at the level of collective memory, it is virtually undetectable.

As far as its place in the public memory is concerned— memory that not only constitutes a community's heritage but is regarded as foundational for a common identity and value system—even less can be said. None of the many significant dates of colonial Italy's prolonged epic have in any way entered the list of holidays or public remembrances and reflections—not dates that celebrate purported glories, nor dates that should recall the certainty that crimes were committed.

For many years, Italian historiography has produced historians who have written about the countries Italy subjugated and brought to the attention of the general public the complexity of the colonial phenomenon, especially from the perspective of the crimes that Italians committed around the world during Italy's eighty years of imperialism. Works such as those of historian and journalist Angelo Del Boca[5] are fundamental in maintaining awareness of the nefarious deeds by which Italians too, albeit with less time and fewer resources than others, managed to stain themselves. Since the turn of the millennium, many works by historians (men and women) have helped broaden the scientific scope and depth of a debate that is fundamental to the evolution of the relationship, in Italy, between history and memory. Analytical essays have proliferated and texts by writers and intellectuals from former colonies, or with family and emotional ties to those realities, have reached the general public.

However, it seems that this past has yet to enter firmly into the daily reality of Italian society. The debate on the colonial legacy, which other Western countries have undertaken—often compelled by their own long-festering social issues and occasionally with less than encouraging outcomes—is only at the embryonic stage in Italy.

A number of obstacles still prevent public opinion from grasping the importance of the debate and making it central and widespread: namely, scant media interest in a subject that seems to have no bearing on the present, mainly because it is not very exploitable in today's political environment (as opposed to other topics such as fascism); and scant public attention to Italy's past attempt to enhance its global influence, which is probably the result of a lack of awareness that our country too left its imperialist "imprint" on the world, indelibly deviating the historical path of the countries it had sought to subjugate and, in turn, changing its own worldview.

In fact, it is commonly believed that Italy was only marginally involved in the great white assault to acquire global wealth, and that, above all, this assault involved very few Italians. In the collective memory, then, this limited involvement, especially after the loss of the colonies following World War II, is sometimes transformed into an implicit sense of disconnection. That Italians adhered "late and poorly" to the assault on other continents is offered as proof that Italians "by their very nature" are not inclined to domination over the Other.

Even when the debate on made-in-Italy colonialism garnered the attention of the general public, concrete efforts were deployed to circumscribe and mitigate any backlash that the awareness of the entirety of such a phenomenon would generate. In the mid-1990s, for example, a controversy raged in the media over the use of poison gas during the war in Ethiopia in 1936. Journalist Indro Montanelli attacked Del Boca's analysis,[6] declaring that as a participant in that conflict, he never saw or heard of the use of chemical weapons. If he did not see or hear of it, then evidently it never happened—bow as we must before the unassailable source. And when the evidence of gassings and violence committed against civilian populations by Italians cannot be disputed, the narrative ascribes these actions to the unfortunately already very large, albeit different, inventory of Fascist crimes. In this way, there is no condemnation of Italian colonialism as such, only of its Mussolinian version.

In essence, in the brief moment when colonial violence is finally being discussed publicly, attention is diverted to the Fascist period, circumscribing Italian responsibilities to the twenty-year Mussolinian period alone. Indeed, in the specific case of the Montanelli-Del Boca diatribe, the discussion is limited to the violence related to "official" military operations in Ethiopia (October 3, 1935 to May 5, 1936). But such an important debate should be extended to cover a period of at least sixty years, even if, paradoxically, Angelo Del Boca's work emphasizes from the outset that the "good people"[7] are "Italian" in a broad sense, and not simply Fascists. Even today, people see a clear distinction—as if the two notions were separated surgically—between aggressive, violent, and Fascist colonialism and the rest of the Italian colonial experience, which, if mentioned at all, was milder, less ferocious, even "humane."

Undoubtedly, Fascism imposed a violently disastrous end to Italian imperialism, but it was nonetheless just one of a number of phases of a phenomenon that was anything but peaceful–from the attempted invasions of Ethiopia in the 1890s, to the Libyan War in 1911-12, to the subsequent years of guerrilla warfare and reprisals. The violence against rebel populations in the Horn of Africa in the late nineteenth century and the massacres of civilians in Tripolitania, Cyrenaica, and Fezzan occurred well before 1922. One can see many more instances of continuity than of disconnection in the overseas policy between liberal Italy and the Fascist regime. Yet, it seems that when it comes to the colonial question, only certain narratives find a place for debate in our country's public arena, thus flattening the complexity of a political, military, cultural, and social movement that characterized the very development of Italy on the international scene.

There are many factors, over the years, that have led an entire country to feel not only blameless, but even detached, from what have been its most enduring contours of foreign policy and international development. We will attempt to analyze these factors, both internal and external, in light of the widespread acquiescence of the population toward the colonial phenomenon during its unfolding (1882-1960), and its almost automatic replacement by an almost unanimous desire to forget it immediately after the end of the process (1960 to the present). A collective amnesia was fostered in large part as a political and cultural choice. When one speaks of colonialism, one's thoughts most easily go to the affairs of powers such as Britain and France or, further back in time, to the Spanish and Portuguese in the Americas.

Yet, for many years, that determination to jump on the European bandwagon to invade the planet is what drove Italy's awareness of its place in the world. Beginning in the 1880s in particular, Italy's status as a great power depended in large part on this very aspect of its foreign policy, characterizing its choices of alliances, its national and international political crises, and the diplomatic victories (few) and defeats (many) of its various governments. It constituted a major part of the country's difficulties in dealing with peace after both World War I and World War II, and for decades to come it influenced its place in the major post-war international organizations, the first among these, the United Nations.

This book is not, nor is it intended as, a history of Italian colonialism. The aim is not to recount the long and painful history of Italy's relationship with the countries that were under its rule for almost a century. Rather, its objective is to analyze the common perception of this past from an economic, social, and cultural point of view.

The events that disrupted the lives of millions of people on several continents, because of Italian imperialism, will be used as examples to illustrate how Italian society perceived colonialism. This book is not a history of massacres perpetrated but not recounted, nor of acts of violence hidden and forgotten, nor of oppressive actions that left few and feeble traces in the memory and conscience of the country. It is not a history of Italy "in Africa" or of any other place the country invaded, occupied, and subdued. On the contrary, it is an attempt to identify the hidden but persistent traces of the impact this subjugation had on the country, its people, and their mindset. The focus of the analysis will be "Africa in Italy," amid the lies, racism, and selective amnesia, following a century and a half of "failed" attempts to face the truth.

An attempt will therefore be made to shed light on the perspective of a country that for a long time adhered to the rhetoric of "foreign lands" and tried to foster it on a global scale; but Italy came late to the endeavour of world conquest and was therefore hindered by all the insecurities of the "latecomer."

As the original Italian version of this book was going to press, news came of the passing of Angelo Del Boca. Del Boca was among the most important journalists, historians, and investigators of memory in twentieth-century Italy. His works paved the way to an understanding of our colonial past and beyond. If many books, this one included, have sought to draw attention to Italy's historical responsibilities, it is also thanks to his tireless work, which is indispensable for our past and our future.

Chapter 1

Departures

Unplanned Birth of an Imperial Power

> The sacred soil of Egypt is invaded
> by the barbaric Ethiopians. Our fields
> Are ravaged... our crops burned... and bold
> Of their easy victory, the predators
> Are already marching onto Thebes!
>
> *– from Scene One, Act One of* Aida
> *by Giuseppe Verdi (1871)*

Each of the European nations that took part in the race to conquer the globe, from the sixteenth-century onward, had its own set of political, economic, and cultural motivations. This chapter focuses on the set of events that led the Kingdom of Italy to its transformation, in just over two decades, from a territorial reality, with still uncertain borders, to the last but nonetheless equally fierce participant in the race to advance Western domination over the rest of the world.

Premise: Why Colonies?

In 1845, a British Royal Navy taskforce near Lagos, in present-day Nigeria, assigned to fighting the slave trade on the Atlantic, intercepted a Genoese ship flying the colours of the Kingdom of Sardinia. Two years later, in 1847, two more

Sardinian vessels were stopped on the same charge of human trafficking. Between 1848 and 1849 there were nearly fifty voyages made between Africa and Brazil by ships under the House of Savoy, which Britain suspected were feeding the slave trade.[1]

The question of why it is important today to discuss Italy's relationship with the colonial world could thus be answered by saying that "Italians" were involved in colonial otherness—and its ugliest expressions, namely slavery—even before Italy itself was formed.

What is it that drives a sovereign state to invade foreign territories, establish outposts, and impose new political, economic, and cultural arrangements? In the case of Italy, there are many reasons why over time and, in particular, between the second half of the nineteenth and the first half of the twentieth centuries, the various governments, whether liberal, fascist, or republican, tried to occupy and build pieces of state outside the peninsula's borders.

Indeed, what is interesting is that almost always, the governments' motivations for promoting the colonial enterprises were different from the reasons these same governments gave the public. At every international forum where Italian policy could be promoted, successive governments felt the need to justify their actions, though these were demonstrably random—for example, a vacuum in international policy, the benevolence of the superpower of the moment, creating improbable expectations for expeditions—and describing all these as "opportunities not to be missed." Even when they were mere exercises in the use of force, such as the occupation of some small island in the Mediterranean, the government and media propaganda machine took care to justify the action by invoking arguments such as, "we are here to civilize; there is an economic advantage; we bring prosperity."

This was a tantalizing premise, which for many Italians created an image of the colony even before it was actually conquered. Then, as often happened, when the hopes in the new conquests were dashed, dreams were replaced by bitterness, and the promise of wealth was substituted with the drudgery of maintaining power.

In the often-wide gap between the hopes cultivated by governments—hopes that were inculcated in the nascent public opinion—and the harsh reality of the colonies lies one of the main reasons for the difficulties of analyzing Italian imperialism historically and give a true "accounting" of colonialism.

We are not invoking an "appraisal" of "Italy in the world" but, rather, an appraisal of the "world in Italy," for "colonialism, far from being a phenomenon circumscribed in the space of European foreign policy or economy, manifests itself as one of the cultural elements on which the different national communities of the old continent were built."[2]

A Bad Start

On November 17, 1869, the Suez Canal was officially opened, with a ceremonial cruise which all the crowned heads of Europe attended. Finally, the Mediterranean was connected to the Red Sea, and ships no longer needed to circumnavigate the entire African continent to reach Asia from Europe. This was a revolution in transportation which, after centuries, restored the Mediterranean as a hub of world trade, a status that had gradually waned since the opening of Atlantic trade routes in the sixteenth century.

On November 15, 1869, two days before French Empress Eugénie, wife of Napoleon III, and Emperor Franz Joseph of Austria sailed their respective yachts through the canal, a critical matter was resolved on the *Nasser Megid*, a much more modest vessel owned by a certain Said-Auadh.[3] Two brothers, Hassan-ben-Ahmad and Ibrahim-ben-Ahmad, co-sultans of Assab, a town on the Eritrean coast of the Red

Sea, "sold and do sell to a Mr Joseph Sapeto the territory between Mount Ganga, Cape Lumah and the two sides thereof; wherefore, the dominion of the said territory shall belong to Mr Joseph Sapeto, as soon as he shall have disbursed the price thereof, they having freely sold it to him, voluntarily and with righteous intention."[4]

Giuseppe Sapeto (1811-1895),[5] who sealed the deal with the two brother sultans of Assab on board the *Nasser Megid*, was an Italian explorer who had long lived in an area between Eritrea and Ethiopia. A scholar of Arabic and African cultures, he was a typical example of a nineteenth-century European interested in Africa. Motivated by a general curiosity about the African continent, he promoted the study of specific locales and their respective culture, all the while having firmly in mind the goal of exploration that would lead to a "profitable civilizing effect"—by the whites in Africa. On that November day in 1869, Sapeto, both a missionary and a businessman, purchased land on Assab Bay on behalf of the Rubattino shipping company, based in Genoa.[6] This was the first act of an overseas land purchase by a company from within the newly formed Kingdom of Italy. For some, it is the starting date of the brief period of Italian "informal imperialism."[7]

The purchase of this portion of coastline was a gamble that the Rubattino Company took ostensibly for economic reasons. Now that the Suez Canal was opened and the Red Sea was about to become one of the most profitable routes in the world, Assab, right on the Red Sea facing the British port of Aden, would become a landing and supply point for Italian steamships connecting the Mediterranean to India, or so the Genoese shipowner dreamed.

This was seen as a clever commercial manoeuvre, initiated by a representative of Italy's fledgling business class. Moreover, on paper it was a forward-looking operation. To have one's very own commercial base right in the middle of such a promising new trade route would have meant, at least in theory, excellent profits. Unfortunately for Rubattino, it was difficult for the Italians to get a foothold in a trade that was monopolized by the British. In addition, the British were better organized, and they controlled both the departure points in Asia and the more prosperous arrival markets in Europe—above all, the ones in Britain. The meagre demand of the small and still undeveloped Italian consumer market did not allow the company to keep the expensive ocean routes in the black, nor cover the costs of maintaining the Assab base. Offers to sell portions of land around the bay[8] came and went for a decade in a desperate attempt to get the trading post off the ground: all to no avail.

Thus, after years of chaos, the Genoese company was faced with two alternatives: ending the agreement with the Sultans of Assab and effectively abandoning the bay, or devolving its rights to someone else, foremost the Italian state. In the spring of 1882, an agreement ceding Assab Bay and its infrastructure to Italy was presented for debate to the Italian Chamber of Deputies, with the aim of transforming what began as a private sale in 1869 into a full-fledged territorial annexation.

A Matter of Prestige

If for the Rubattino company the cession was motivated by economic difficulties, for the Italian government taking it over was mainly a matter of prestige. The decision by the executive branch was endorsed by a sizable parliamentary consensus.

The years around 1882 were a peculiar time for Italian foreign policy: a year earlier there had been the so-called "slap of Tunis," that is, the French occupation of Tunisia. It was an imposition of the status quo by force that annihilated any ambitions that the young Kingdom of Italy might have had on the southern coast of the Mediterranean. The shock produced by Italy's impotence against the French caused the fall of the government of Benedetto Cairoli (1825-1889), who was replaced by Agostino Depretis (1813-1887). It would also be one of the main reasons for Italy entering into the Triple Alliance with Germany and Austria-Hungary[9] that same year. This was a diplomatic revolution with paradoxical features. Austria still possessed territories inhabited by Italian-speakers that Italy coveted as part of the fatherland. As such, Austria was Italy's main antagonist on the Balkan chessboard. The purpose of such a radical move was ostensibly to bring the country out of a dangerous diplomatic isolation, demonstrated by the fact that, faced with the French act of force, no European country had taken Italy's side.

In such a sensitive situation, in which Italian diplomacy was still smarting from the French aggression and the kingdom's image was faltering, the very idea of abandoning the only shred of non-European territory in Italian hands, albeit private, was unacceptable. The African outpost over which the tri-colour flag already flew, if only for commercial purposes, had to be maintained at all costs, especially since letting Rubattino fail in Assab would mean acknowledging what was already believed in many European capitals: Italians did not have the makings of an imperial power. Therefore, with very broad support from the political class, the Rubattino company was generously liquidated and Assab was transformed from a commercial base into an Italian possession, thus saving the company's accounts and Italian prestige on the international scene all at once.

Of course, the annexation process could not have been carried out without the prior consent of the colonial superpower of the time, Great Britain, which had every intention of maintaining an iron grip on its supply routes. Italy's seizure of Assab was possible only by prior agreement with

Britain, which saw the Italian presence as a way to weaken Egypt's already precarious hold on the coastline of the Red Sea; and to prevent those lands from falling into the hands of more formidable competitors than tiny Italy, namely France.

Following an exchange of official notes with the then Italian foreign minister, Pasquale Stanislao Mancini (1817-1888), the British approved the proposed annexation in February 1882.[10] This was certainly not a shining entry in the so-called scramble for Africa,[11] far from it. As historian Nicola Labanca pointed out, "London led Rome by the hand into the Red Sea,"[12] making Italy's version of colonialism a by-product of Britiain's.

Even after 1882, Italian expansionist ambitions would have to contend with the actual powers in the various world theatres. In the end, it was Britain itself, during World War II, who would oust Italy from all the colonial possessions it had accumulated over time.

But for the time being, the operation allowed the government of the so-called Historical Left to record a foreign policy win and present the acquisition of Assab as an act of international prestige. Prestige, as we shall see, would be one of the main drivers of virtually all Italian colonial adventures—and misfortunes.

How Do I Sell You Occupation?
I: I Am "Bringing Civilization"

But the Italian government's acquisition of the Assab base and its formal transformation into a colony could not be presented to the public (however narrow a cohort it was at the time), neither as the government rescue of a failed business nor as meagre consolation prize for the loss of Tunis. Officially, from what is revealed in the text of the parliamentary debate that preceded passage of the law, the reasons given were other: above all, the debate centred on the desire to contribute to the peaceful "civilization" of the populace.

When the Honourable Alberto Cavalletto, from Padua (1813-1897), took the floor in parliament, he declared:

> ... I recommend that we go there with ideas of true development, and not with ideas of conquest, with ideas of civilizing those populations that will freely want to join us, make life with our nationals, but not with ideas of violently superimposing ourselves on the natives.[13]

The drafter of the bill, Vincenzo Picardi (1828-1890), responded confidently that it was the government's intention to carry out civilizing work, if not, indeed,

> ... as far as possible, adapt ourselves to the inclinations, to the habits of the indigenous people with whom we must forge fraternal relations, and not relations as conquerors and conquered. [...] So that the work of civilization may succeed, it is first and foremost necessary to respect history, religious sentiments, customs, and support, within certain limits, the ambitions of the peoples to whom the prodigious benefits of civilization must be brought. Demolishing existing traditions and customs and abruptly imposing novel institutions that are neither understood nor appreciated, and entrusting the colonial hold entirely to new men unknown to the natives, would create an element of distrust and deeply offend the pride of those races who are steadfastly attached to their customs.[14]

These are truly forward-looking aims, consistent with the nineteenth-century notion of the export of civilization—a flattering undertaking. Moreover, there is no reason to dismiss these statements as mere posturing, on the contrary. A segment of the country's intellectual elite was convinced that it was one of white society's duties to civilize the world. In Italy, as in the rest of Europe, the set of theories on white racial and cultural superiority, encompassed by Rudyard Kipling's famous 1899 poem, "The White Man's Burden,"[15] were widespread, and they constituted a strong basis for taking colonial action. It is no coincidence that the Italian overseas adventures of the late nineteenth century were all undertaken by governments of the so-called Historical Left. For this "progressive" wing of the royal parliament, it was perfectly logical to advocate for domestic policies such as the expansion of suffrage and school reform and, in foreign policy, for the civilization and development of "primitive populations." Furthermore, the politics of power, when presented under the cloak of progress, also found support among the masses. As historian Eric J. Hobsbawm summarizes, "...it is impossible to deny that the idea of superiority to, and domination over, a world of dark skins in remote places was genuinely popular, and thus benefited the politics of imperialism."[16] Unfortunately, however, these noble proposals for the future of Italian Africa clashed almost immediately with the reality of racist, rapacious, and bloodthirsty rule.

Men who were unsuitable for the management of the colony, almost all of them soldiers, were put in key administrative posts; without adequate training, difficulties quickly emerged. In 1891, whispers of violence and oppression reached the ears of Italian public opinion. Various episodes of torture and violence against people were recounted, and there was talk of targeted killings orchestrated by the Italian commander of Massawa's indigenous police, Royal Carabinieri lieutenant Dario Livraghi.[17] The purpose of these crimes, ostensibly disguised as police operations, appeared to be Livraghi's own greed—enriching himself by seizing the assets of the murdered local Eritrean elders.

The trial received extensive coverage in the media, not least because Livraghi, who at first fled to Switzerland, was eventually acquitted along with his accomplices; but also because the blatant violence, impossible to conceal, was attributed to his indigenous troops. The trial appeared to many news commentators as having been fixed, and its conclusion was greeted with anger in anti-colonialist circles.

Generally speaking, the "Livraghi scandal" cast the colonial venture in a bad light and, in many quarters, people were beginning to talk about the possibility of abandoning the colonies on the Red Sea. At the moment, at least, it was not yielding the hoped-for economic benefits; on the contrary, it was casting disgrace on the armed forces. Thus, the export of "civilization" did not have a very auspicious start.

How Do I Sell You Occupation?
II: "I Offer You a Great Banquet"

Alongside the moral imperatives, there were other impulses that accompanied the opening of a space defined in parliament by the foreign minister, Pasquale Stanislao Mancini (1817-1888) himself, as "politically Italian."[18] The idea was always to foster economic activities that not only repaid the efforts, but that also created revenue for the state.

The allure of overseas wealth appealed to many, and the government was convinced that it could provide the right protection and guarantees for private enterprise to take root, not least because the colonial system developed in other countries seemed to have brought prosperity to those powers. The wealth and power of Britain and France seemed to confirm the fact that the colonies were a profitable investment.

For a long time, voices in Italy spoke of the marvels, especially in Africa, that would make everyone rich. As early as 1865, Giuseppe Sapeto himself, the former missionary who signed the contract for Assab on behalf of the Rubattino company, wrote an essay, "L'Italia e il Canale di Suez, Operetta Popolare,"[19] on the benefits of transcontinental trade. On the title page of the work, dedicated to the Chambers of Commerce of the Kingdom of Italy, he indicated that "the only interest I have in dedicating this pamphlet to you, most illustrious gentlemen, is my desire, as it is yours, to make our homeland rich in trade, prosperous in industry, powerful in virtue."[20]

Throughout the nineteenth century, European travellers and explorers returned to Europe with tales of exotic and mysterious places that were seemingly full of treasures and raw materials. There was a widespread belief that Africa in particular was a "virgin" continent to be explored, and especially exploited. An enterprising and modern entrepreneurial class could not pass up the opportunity to take part in the banquet.

However, in the last two decades of the nineteenth century the Italian entrepreneurial class was not even remotely comparable to its English or French counterpart. A chronic lack of capital greatly restricted the possibilities for commercial expansion, and the Italian market was far less developed than that of other European countries. Finally, state structures, which elsewhere effectively supported business ventures, simply did not exist in Italy. The Rubattino Company illustrated this point—a good idea, on paper, of an Italian company trying to profit from international trade, but falling into a bottomless pit. The only solution remained massive state intervention. But many saw this merely as growing pains. In the government's view, the colonies would soon sustain themselves, and even contribute to the country's wealth. To achieve this, it was necessary to convince private individuals to invest.

However, there was one fact that even the government's determination could not escape: Assab, with its few square kilometres of land between the Red Sea and the desert, was anything but a lush paradise for entrepreneurs. As soon as they acquired that first bit of Africa, the Italians realized that it was nowhere near enough to sustain the dreams of grandeur and wealth being envisaged.

So there it was, right from the start, the public narrative around the first, measly Italian colony took the form of "just the beginning." Assab was no longer an Italic enclave on African soil, but a bridgehead for the eventual conquest of an entire continent. Thus, what had been envisioned as a peaceful adventure turned into a feverish military operation to expand the territory. The stretch of coastline under Italian control was militarized, becoming a base to support inland incursions. Maintaining the port cost a lot and yielded almost nothing, as would have been evident by simply glancing at the accounts of the Rubattino shipping company. However, abandoning it was not an option, for reasons of prestige already described. So, as often happens in games of chance, after a bad first hand the player doubles down.

From Assab to Massawa, from Massawa to Asmara: The "First Colony" Is Born

If Assab fell into Italian government hands through a series of murky negotiations between private businessmen and local sultans, the port of Massawa, a far richer and more desirable trading post, came under the Italian orbit through a fortuitous international entanglement. Neighbouring Sudan, under formal Egyptian control, was in open revolt, and the government in Cairo, in theory independent but in fact stage-managed by Britain, was decidedly weak. Some Red Sea ports owned by Egypt, including Massawa, were dangerously unprotected. The risk was great that some European power, namely France, would take possession in a coup. For this reason, British diplomacy again proposed to Italy that it expand its sphere and occupy the port of Massawa. Evidently, for the British government, the Italians posed no real threat and, indeed, just like the Egyptians, they could be used (as pawns rather than protagonists) in the game of the great onslaught on Africa. So it was that, at the invitation of the British in 1885, after a brief period of cohabitation (the Italians landed on February 5, while the last Egyptian soldiers left on December 2), an Italian military brigade took effective possession of the port city.

Without any groundwork in the media to shape public opinion, the sudden occupation of Massawa was difficult to understand. An editorial in the July 20, 1885, issue of *Corriere della Sera*[21] remarked: "Why Italy went to Massawa, we do not pretend to understand, and many among us will not presume to understand either. Indeed, some dare say that perhaps even the government that approved the expedition does not know exactly." But the government's line of justification was now overtly imperialistic: Assab was not sustainable as a single colony, too small and too far away. The addition of Massawa could guarantee an economic return, as well as strengthen the Italian presence in the area—an area that was increasingly described as desirable and, above all, "available."

In fact, not even possession of Massawa could guarantee an economic return, for the same reasons that prevented the development of Assab: too little traffic, too much competition from other European posts in the area. These occupations were justifiable only as bases, not so much for international commerce, but as ports to funnel wealth from the rich hinterland. The Ethiopian plateau, at the time hosting the seat of an independent, multi-ethnic empire that was virtually unknown to the world, provided a possible path for the expression of Italy's ambitions. It was free of "obligations" towards Europe, boundless, and therefore imagined as extremely rich.

After 1885, Italy's efforts to expand were largely explained to the public as attempts to consolidate colonial positions, rationalize the structures of colonial holdings, and protect successive places of interest. This was the reason given for occupying Asmara, a city in the interior, away from Massawa. The same reason was given for erecting defensive forts on the way to the highlands, though these were met with increasingly intense local resistance. In a sort of vicious circle, more and more money and energy were expended in the hope of getting the Italian "African dream" off the ground—a dream now decidedly structured within an imperialist impulse. On January 1, 1890, by royal decree,[22] the possessions accumulated thus far through the continuous aggregation of adjacent territories were organized into a unitary colony, which took the name of "Eritrea."[23]

Chapter 2

Arrivals

Colonial Failures—A New Lie for Every Conquest

Do you know where the most fertile soil is found?
Do you know where the most magical sun glows?
On the sea that binds us to Golden Africa
The star of Italy points us to a treasure
Points us to a treasure!

Giovanni Corvetto and Colombino Arona
"To Tripoli" (song, 1911)

If the start of the Italian colonial adventure occurred rather fortuitously—the result of an unforeseen set of circumstances that favoured conquest more than the full fruit of political calculus, the construction of the economic and political motivations that fuelled the momentum of overseas enterprises can instead be ascribed to the desire of the various governments, and of culturally or economically powerful individuals, who pushed the country along an imperialist path.

This chapter focuses on the set of public narratives put forward over time to justify, in the eyes of the country, the efforts to consolidate and expand Italian overseas possessions.

From "Prosperous Eritrea" to Abyssinia, to the (Failed) Conquest of a Country of "Savages"

The creation of the Eritrean colony and the establishment of direct rule through the creation of an ad hoc bureaucracy were not the end point of Italian colonial policy but, paradoxically, a new beginning. This formalization should have provided greater stability, but in reality, the borders of the possessions in the west remained deliberately undefined. Italian authorities moved quickly to clarify which settlements were under their direct control, and they began to exercise direct rule through the administration of justice and attempts to tax the population. But they refused to specify where in the Ethiopian plateau their claims officially ended. From 1890 onwards, populations in the interior resisted the invasion or simply remained loyal to the local rulers, resulting in a succession of border conflicts.

But the Italian colonial authorities already had the Ethiopian Empire in their sights as the next area in which to expand. This last plot of "available" land on the African continent was a vast territory inhabited by multiple ethnic groups, often at war with one another. The vicissitudes of history further complicated Italy's dreams of glory. After decades of internal strife, a convergence of events would see the rise of one of the greatest political figures of nineteenth-century Africa, Emperor[1] Menelik II.[2] Power over the entire territory would soon be concentrated in his hands, thus putting a damper on Italy's expansionist impulses.

Italy's desire to bite into the most prosperous morsel remaining in the "African banquet" inexorably transformed the Eritrean colony, slowly turning it into an outpost where power was put in the hands of the military and where the legal system, infrastructures, and social policies were subordinated to a strategy of aggression towards Ethiopia.[3] The early governors of the colony were military men, as were the vast majority of personnel arriving in the territory between 1890 and 1896.

The occupiers' first tangible efforts to involve the local population was to recruit them as soldiers. As early as 1885, the first one hundred Eritrean irregular soldiers were used to support the occupation of Massawa.[4] These units fought alongside the Italians in the many border clashes. In 1891, just one year after the creation of the colonial government, the " Royal Corps of Eritrean Colonial Troops"[5] was officially established. In fact, the only "local resource" that the occupiers seemed to be able to exploit was the military skills of the occupied. They were labelled Askari,[6] a term that would soon enter the Italian language with a pejorative connotation. Used as expendable troops in many theatres of war on the African continent, Askari were, for almost the entire colonial period, one of the few ways in which the inhabitants of the colonies earned mentions in the national narrative. In parades of both liberal and Fascist Italy, they were exhibited as curiosities who, through their uniforms and an overstated rhetoric, evoked a fascination with the exotic and implied a savage violence.

Though technically unprepared, the Italian government continued to pursue an aggressive and, at times, openly contemptuous policy towards its Ethiopian neighbour, who it considered not up to the challenge.

In 1889, as soon as the colonial governorship was installed, a treaty of friendship and trade was proposed to the Ethiopian Empire. It was signed in the Ethiopian town of Uccialli, which gave the treaty its name. In reality, the text of the agreement was a rather clumsy ruse to deceive the newly installed Emperor Menelik II and the government in Addis Ababa[7] into accepting a protectorate over the entire Ethiopian region. The text of the treaty was drafted in the languages of the two contracting parties, Italian and Amharic. But the two versions diverged in one fundamental point: in Article 17, the Italian version declared: "His Majesty the King of Kings of Ethiopia consents to use the government of His Majesty the King of Italy for all business dealings he may have with other powers or governments."[8]

Menelik II, therefore, had ostensibly agreed to be represented by Italy in its foreign relations. In the Amharic version the verb that in Italian was rendered as "consents" simply meant "may." That is, the Emperor of Ethiopia would only use Italian diplomacy as an intermediary, if necessary. A single word, purposely translated incorrectly, allowed the Italian government to assert that it had the right to speak on Ethiopia's behalf in international forums. This was a clear attempt to deceive a country evidently seen as too backward and too unsophisticated diplomatically to notice the difference.

As soon as Menelik II discovered how the treaty was being presented in European capitals he repudiated it, reaffirming the full independence of his empire. On August 24, 1890, the emperor wrote to Umberto I, King of Italy, to request the revision of the Italian version of the treaty. He also wrote to other European sovereigns, including Queen Victoria of England, to publicly denounce Italy's claims.[9] The hope of deceiving the "Abyssinian savages" foundered miserably, and it gave Menelik II an international audience to present himself as strong and independent.

Eritrea, a garrison colony, remained on permanent alert for another five years, with constant border clashes. What were dismissed in the national press as minor border skirmishes or misunderstandings (if they were mentioned at all), were in reality part of an actual guerrilla war, which Italy tried to fight mainly with colonial troops. The use of Italian soldiers was risky because, in the event of defeat, it would be difficult to cover up the news. The dead white officers and soldiers had families in Italy, and their killing would have to be investigated and justified through official reports. The death of Eritreans in the service of the Royal Italian Army, on the other hand, did not make the news.

For instance, there are streets and squares dedicated to the 500 Italians (430, actually) who died in the Battle of Dògali, on January 26, 1887, including "Piazza of the Five Hundred" opposite Rome's Termini Station,[10] but there is not a single monument to the thousands of colonial and allied troops who died under the Italian flag.

The climate of permanent conflict was obviously not reported back home. Instead, reports were widely circulated that a model colony was being built on the Red Sea, in spite of occasional disruptions on the western border due to the primitive and quarrelsome Ethiopian neighbours, with whom it would be appropriate to come to terms once and for all.

For this reason, there was widespread disbelief when news reached Italy on March 3, 1896, that a major battle had taken place two days earlier between Italian soldiers trying to break into the Ethiopian plateau and Menelik II's army. When the "Battle of Abba Carima" (later called the "Battle of Adua") was reported in the papers, the little stretch of land occupied by the Italians on the Red Sea gripped public opinion. Until then, Eritrean affairs had been confined to foreign policy circles. Now, however, the newspapers published maps of the Eritrean-Ethiopian border on the front pages in an attempt to familiarize readers with the places where so many Italian soldiers had died. The clash between 17,000 Italian army soldiers (10,000 of whom were Italians) and the army of the Negus, comprised of over 100,000 men, was a massacre. "During the battle, 289 officers, 4600 non-commissioned officers and soldiers, and about 1000 Askari were killed. About 1000 Eritreans and 1900 Italians were captured by the enemy."[11]

Francesco Crispi, leader of the Historical Left and prime minister, had staked his hopes on making the conquest of Ethiopia the qualitative leap needed for Italy to become a great power. The full stop encountered in the field, labelled as a "defeat" at first, was re-categorized as a "rout" when the number of dead, wounded, and missing arrived. In addition, it led to the fall of the Crispi government and the end of many of Italy's ambitions in Africa. Above all, it marked the beginning of a great inferiority complex for Italy vis-à-vis the other actors on the stage of international imperialism.[12] The hitherto divided anti-colonial movement—that included socialist proponents of pacifist and egalitarian internationalism[13] as well as elements of the liberal middle and upper-middle classes who saw the colonies as a waste of resources—was strengthened. After Adua, the idea that colonialism was a harmful pursuit prevailed in the sphere of the country's nascent public opinion. A shift occurred: pro-colonialist governments' condemnations of anti-colonialists as "sympathizers of the barbarians"[14] were replaced by a brutal disenchantment with an adventure that many already considered a failure.

It was because of Adua that Eritrea, presented for at least a decade as an "outpost" against Ethiopia, needed to change vocation. The "door" to the empire had been violently shut in the face of Italy's colonialists: the reason for owning that strip of land on the Red Sea had to be totally reinvented.

"Virgin and Fertile," the First Colony for People

The violence with which Italy's claims to the Ethiopian Empire came to a halt forced the government to radically rethink the role of the Eritrean colony in national and international affairs. Expensive to maintain and decidedly unproductive, as it could no longer serve as a gateway to Ethiopia's alleged wealth, Eritrea became the focus of a propaganda campaign in the latter years of the nineteenth century aimed at making it a "colony for people." Following the French example in Algeria, the idea was to make the Red Sea possession a destination for the tens of thousands of

Italians who were emigrating from the country every year. The notion had been in the air for some time. As early as 1890, member of Parliament Leopoldo Franchetti had been sent by Prime Minister Crispi to visit the colony to evaluate possible forms of development. In his report upon his return,[15] Franchetti highlighted the agricultural potential of the area, extolling, perhaps hyperbolically, its fertility. In actual fact, the potential described by Franchetti referred largely to a territory in the Ethiopian highlands, which in point of fact Italy did not control and was a cause of the constant clashes with the Ethiopians. After 1896, when economics became the justification for the colonial adventure and agriculture was made the focus for "exporting settlers" to Africa, the results were disappointing.

Despite recruitment efforts and constant propaganda campaigns to "sell" Italians on the idea of an agricultural Eden on the Red Sea, the problem was that millions of Italian emigrants were choosing to try their luck in destinations already set in their imagination. North and South America were attracting hundreds of thousands of Italians, while Italian governments laboured to present the Red Sea colony as a viable alternative to overseas migration. Between 1891 and 1900, 283,000 people left Italy. The following decade would see another 603,000 Italians leave the country.[16] Of these, only a few hundred chose "fertile and virgin" Eritrea, and a good number of these soon returned home. The colony proved even less appealing for entrepreneurs and adventurers. In 1899, Europeans in Eritrea, excluding military personnel, totalled 1741. This number included Italians, Austrians, French, Greeks, and Swedes—in a local population of 330,000.[17] These figures were a far cry from the idea of a colony for people. Yet, this is Eritrea as it continued to be portrayed in the press and how it was administered by successive governors.

To introduce industrial agriculture, the Italian occupiers undertook a vast campaign to transform the territories. They seized land and belongings in villages accused of sedition or of collaboration with their Ethiopian neighbours. Furthermore, they proclaimed vast areas as "no man's land," which allowed the state to put these areas up for sale. Between 1893 and 1895, following a series of decrees, 400,000 hectares of farmland were seized by the Italian administration.[18] More would follow. This was land used primarily for grazing by nomadic and semi-nomadic peoples, who were ousted from their thousand-year-old pastures to benefit a few large agricultural ventures subsidized by the colonial state.

Over the years, this imposition altered the very profile of the colony, depriving thousands of inhabitants of their primary livelihood and destroying the self-sustaining balance of the Eritrean economy. One of the reasons that, over time, Eritrea became fertile ground for recruitment by the Italian colonial army is that there was no other way for the local population to survive than to have its young men join the army.

Despite efforts to somehow make Eritrea useful and profitable for Italy, the colony's budget produced a deficit throughout the entire period of Italian occupation, especially after 1896. There were no major activities to be taxed, and industrial agricultural production did not take root except through heavy public intervention. Even protectionist policies initiated at the end of the nineteenth century failed to make locally produced goods competitive.

Without a clear purpose, appeal or prospects, Eritrea, which became known as "the primitive colony," remained a black hole in the state budget and a failure on the so-called civilization front.

Somalia: *Terra Incognita*

While Italy's Red Sea possessions struggled to get off the ground and caused more headaches than they were worth, the government, once again urged on and supported by Great Britain, decided to open a new front. On February 8, 1889, a treaty was signed that recognized the Italian protectorate of the Sultanate of Hobyo, a statelet on the shores of the Indian Ocean. On April 7 of the same year, a similar treaty was signed with the Sultanate of Migiurtinia, which had sovereignty over the coastline on the Horn of Africa between the Red Sea and the Indian Ocean. Again, as in Eritrea, this was an operation of "sub-contracted colonialism" or colonialism by proxy by the British. Italy was increasingly being made a pawn in the real imperial game taking place between France and Britain. The pretext of the operation was obvious even to the general public. Italy went into Somalia because Her Majesty's British government liked it that way. Nevertheless, this subalternity was seen by Italian diplomatic circles as an opportunity to slip into the drawing rooms of the diplomacy "that matters," even if the Foreign Office's attitude towards Italy was anything but "one of equals," judging by the bilateral agreements and special authorizations to conquer.

But this was not a problem for the Italian government, which took advantage of the favourable climate to extend its control, in theory, over almost 1000 kilometres of coastline, between the Indian Ocean and the Red Sea.

Protectorate agreements are often perceived differently by the parties involved. While the Italian Foreign Ministry considered the areas in question as being under its exclusive jurisdiction, the local sultans saw the protectorate literally as a form of protection and, above all, as a way to legitimize their status vis-à-vis neighbouring adversaries. In particular, they saw it as having secured a European ally in their disputes with, for example, their Ethiopian rival. The 1889 agreements did not alter the actual situation on the ground, and the Italian commitment was, ostensibly, less important than in Eritrea. The decision was made that Italy would establish its presence in the new possessions via private commercial enterprises. In 1893, Vincenzo Filonardi (1853-1916), a military man, politician, and "merchant trader,"[19] who already had interests in the not-too-distant Zanzibar, was entrusted with the exploitation of the agricultural, commercial and population opportunities of the acquired territories.

This was clearly an act of disengagement by the government, given the already massive difficulties it was encountering in trying to colonize Eritrea. Filonardi's company was given a 300,000-lira-per-year subsidy, and Filonardi himself was conferred absolute civil and military authority. Three years later, the agreement had yielded practically nothing. As a result, on April 15, 1896, the task of running the colony was entrusted to another company, the *Società Anonima Italiana del Benadir*,[20] created expressly for this purpose, which took over from Filonardi. This new private agreement was approved by a special law[21] upon its renewal in 1899. The law now named after the company's owners: Silvio Benigno Crespi (1868-1944), one of the richest and most active entrepreneurs in the Italian cotton industry, Giorgio Mylius (1870-1935), also a wealthy cotton merchant, and Angelo Carminati (1856-1934), an entrepreneur with interests in various sectors, from chemistry to textiles.[22]

The law that renewed the agreement obliged the *Società Anonima Italiana del Benadir*,

> ... to foster the civil and commercial growth of the colony and give a detailed accounting of these activities to the Italian government, which will always retain the right to supervise the work of the Società. The Società will also have to promote, in the most opportune ways, the economic life of the lands it has been granted, carrying out all the works it deems necessary for this purpose.[23]

Conversely,

... from May 10, 1898 to April 30, 1910, the Italian Government will pay the Società the annual sum of 400,000 gold francs. From May 1, 1910 to July 16, 1946, it will pay the Società the annual sum of 350,000 gold francs. These sums are for both the maintenance of the existing posts and for those which the Società might thereafter establish.[24]

This was a fair bit of hard currency, sufficient, the government believed, to secure the establishment an "informal imperialism" based on the model of the British East India Company in 1857. Article 4 of the law stated that:

The Government can use the Società, and shall regularly cause it to hold the sum necessary for the payment of the annuities due to the Sultans of Hobyo and Alula, totalling 3600 M.T. thalers;[25] and this for as long as the Government has such an obligation to the said sultans.[26]

This made explicit what was already known to insiders in Italy and abroad: the dominion over Somali lands was not a submission by the local sultans. Rather, the Italians were paying, in hard currency, for the opportunity to do commerce in the region. In return, the Somali leaders earned the protection of a more technologically advanced and better equipped military that, moreover, already had a running tab with their dangerous neighbour, the Ethiopian Empire.

Although the agreement was presented in European capitals and in Italian public opinion as a form of direct influence, the Somali sultans saw it as nothing more than a trade deal and alliance that Italy, moreover, was paying for. In fact, this type of pact between European powers and non-European territories was not uncommon and was usually the prelude to more substantial economic involvement. The belief was that, in a short time, the revenues from the protectorates would far exceed the tribute left in the hands of the local sovereigns.

Unfortunately for successive Italian governments, the plan to commercially break into the Horn of Africa did not materialize, as the *Società Anonima Italiana del Benadir* failed to establish any viable businesses or stimulate any degree of economic activity.

The entrepreneurs involved, who were mainly interested in agricultural exploitation, acted like masters over the local population, to the point of provoking bloody riots. In actual fact, the means at their disposal were limited and poorly employed, inviting the phrase "poor people's colonialism."[27] Ninety percent of the company's expenditures were for the military, which was needed to ensure control and security for the Italians.[28] The cotton company adventure in Somalia ended in disaster, with the revocation of the concession in 1903, and credible accusations of embezzlement and even slavery against the industrialists.[29]

At the trial, the company's top executives were acquitted, as often happened to Italians tried in Italy for crimes committed in Africa. But the damage to the image of Italian business overseas and to the colonial cause itself was enormous. The state was forced to take direct control of its Somali dependencies, and in 1905 it created an administrative structure for the territories on the coast of the Indian Ocean with regulations similar to those in Eritrea.[30] In 1908, the territories were united based on the linguistic model of the neighbouring British colony of Somaliland, and given the name of "Italian Somalia."[31] Italy's second colony in Africa was born.

But, instead of the glories of civilization, the newspapers were full of reports of border clashes and, above all, scandals. The idea began to take hold that these possessions were nothing more than expensive propaganda tools. Despite the creation of Italian colonial associations that favoured colonization, opposition to the Italian commitment in Africa became ever stronger—in the public domain as well as in parliament. As in other European countries, in the early twentieth century, the Kingdom of Italy saw the rise of its own anti-colonial movement, fuelled not only by ethics—a repudiation of the imperialist ethos—but also, and above all, driven by the evident futility and non-viability of the system.[32]

Somalia, which was even less economically viable than Eritrea, fared even worse than the first colony in inspiring the collective imagination. Paradoxically, it would be the strip of Africa to remain under Italian control the longest—until July 1, 1960. Throughout its status as an Italian colony, it remained a mostly mysterious land, the names of its cities barely known. The portrayal of its unique identity was lost, indistinguishable from the thousands of ways of recounting an Africa that Italians never really understood.

To China, to Carry the White Man's Burden

The witlessness of the Italian imperialist movement was clearly demonstrated by a series of colonial gambles taken without the slightest idea of what a possible development plan for the new "Italian outposts in the world" might be. The case of the Italian concession in the Far East and the vicissitudes that led the Kingdom of Italy to conquer a patch of the Chinese Empire are a classic example of an opportunistic attempt to build a prestigious foreign policy at the expense of a medium-to-long-term economic logic.[33]

By the end of the nineteenth century, the continuous abuses and violations of Chinese sovereignty, mainly by the British and Russians, led to the outbreak of an anti-Western revolt in China.[34] The unrest, which began in 1898, was triggered by China's humiliating situation of vassalage and the rise of the Han nationalist movement. The uprising was centred around various Chinese martial arts youth organizations and was thus dubbed the "Boxer Rebellion" by the Western press. The uprising, which condemned the subservience of the imperial court and state officials to the Westerners, who were stripping the country of its wealth, set vast regions of the empire ablaze.

A series of agreements that would go down in history as the "unequal treaties"[35] had been forced on Beijing. But a growing desire for a national riposte began to take hold, and called for the Old Empire to rid itself of foreigners. To avert the risk of losing its hold on the Qing Empire, the British, who had the largest economic interests in that part of Asia and had imposed a sort of protectorate over the Chinese government, decided to act. Their plan was to organize a bona fide international mission to defend Western interests which, in fact, meant their own.

The act of extending the defence of the Chinese status quo to a Western coalition was taken mainly because, at that time, British resources were already being absorbed by the war against the Boers in South Africa.[36] By labelling the Chinese uprising as anti-European, the British government managed to turn an act of repression against a subjugated people into a struggle to defend civilization.

The main victims of the resulting xenophobic violence were Western missionaries and Chinese converts to Christianity. In European and American newspapers, the expedition advocated by London immediately took on the jingoistic jargon of a real crusade of white civilization against yellow barbarism. Even the Italian newspapers, especially in the aftermath of the government's decision to take part in the intervention, were filled with reports of violence and massacres against mostly Chinese converts and Europeans:

> June 16, evening. A telegraph was just received from London: "This, just in from Shanghai. Information received from Tientsin tonight confirms that fires were set in the eastern part of the city. Four churches—three British and one American— and numerous houses belonging to foreigners were set ablaze.

The connection was interrupted when telegraph poles were set on fire; a train with food and ammunition for the international detachment could not reach Langfang and was forced to turn back." This retreat was confirmed by another dispatch from Shanghai. From Tientsin, June 16: News from Peking confirms that numerous local converts and servants of Europeans were massacred on Thursday by Boxers in the eastern quarter. The Catholic cathedral in Beijing was set on fire.[37]

This aspect of international propaganda is crucial to understanding the otherwise nebulous reasons for the Italian government's enthusiastic entry into the war. The Kingdom of Savoy had no special interests to protect in the Celestial Empire. There were no noteworthy trading posts, and direct trade with that part of Asia was insignificant. There was a token diplomatic representation with a small garrison of sailors, which like other European missions, hardly came under threat.

However, the suppression of the Boxer Rebellion by military muscle was motivated by more than just economic interests or the desire to rescue captive diplomats. It was actually a full display of racist power against a world under European, imperialist and white domination. In his infamous speech to soldiers leaving for China, which has gone down in history as the "Hunnenrede"—the Hun Speech, Emperor Wilhelm II of Germany motivated his troops thus:

Act according to traditional Prussian steadfastness! Prove yourselves Christians by joyfully confronting the pagans! May honour and fame accompany your insignia and your arms... There is no forgiveness, there are no prisoners! Just as one thousand years ago the Huns, under King Attila, made a formidable name for themselves that resonates in tradition and in legend to this day, may the name "German" acquire through you such a reputation in China for one thousand years to come, so that a Chinese will never again even dare to look askance at a German.[38]

To participate in this punitive action was to be recognized as a legitimate player; this is the reason many within the Italian government rejoiced when the British called on the international powers, Italy among them, to counter the revolt. It was the longed-for assignment for Italians as standard-bearers of civilization. For the public who read about the terrible massacres perpetrated against Chinese Christians, intervention was not only desirable, it was necessary. Supporting the progress of civilization evidently went hand in hand with the spreading of Christianity.

On July 5, 1900, the government approved the dispatch of a contingent of 2000 soldiers to the Far East, with the task of defending Italian interests in China—though hardly anyone, in the newspapers or in parliament, could identify these interests concretely.

However, many understood the historical importance of the moment for Italy and its honour as a great power. The July 21, 1900, edition of *Corriere della Sera* reprinted a series of moving telegram exchanges between a family of patriots and the king, after the expedition was already on its way:

> A letter from Stilo (Reggio Calabria) received this morning contained a copy of the following telegrams exchanged in recent days between brothers Achille and Raffaele Fazzari (who have thus written enviable pages in the history of our *Risorgimento*) and the King. Mongiana, July 15, 1900. To His Majesty King Umberto, Rome. Sire. We have six sons fit for war. If Your Highness would deign to order them to leave for China to defend the honour of the Fatherland, we would be happy to do so. ACHILLE and RAFFAELE FAZZARI.

The Court responded to this profession of loyalty and patriotism thus:

> Quirinale Palace, Rome, July 16, 1900. To Hon. Achille and Raffaele Fazzari, Mongiana. The most patriotic offer made by Your Lordships to His Highness the King in yesterday's telegram is equal to that of the ancient devotion to Italy and to the

Dynasty, which you all have shown, from all time, such ample proof. The August Sovereign therefore thanks them for the confirmation given to him and sends them cordial greetings.[39]

This call to national honour, as presented in the press, clearly revealed that international commitments were being assumed precisely for the glory of the nation. Between 1900 and 1901, the Italian expeditionary force, together with soldiers from the other imperial states, namely Great Britain, the United States, Russia, France, Germany, Austria-Hungary, and Japan (a sort of G8 *ante litteram*, which were in fact known as "the Eight Nations Alliance"), fought to reconquer a number of rebel strongholds.

Once the nationalists were defeated, the Chinese government accepted Western tutelage and granted the victorious powers further benefits in certain sectors of its economy. The important port city of Tientsin, overlooking the Gulf of Bohai in the Yellow Sea, was divided between the occupiers. Even Italy, which had paid a tribute of eighteen dead soldiers, could sit at the peace table. The "Tianjin Concession, " established on September 7, 1901 and turned over to Italy, consisted of just under forty-six hectares of land along the river, adjacent to the city's port, much of it marshland that until then had been used as a cemetery.

This was a decidedly paltry reward. The British, by comparison, occupied 388 hectares of the city in the port area, with well-developed infrastructures. Meanwhile, with no economic prospects on the horizon, the land in the Italian concession would have to be reclaimed and made suitable for the construction of wharves. Above all, Italians would have to shoulder the burden of building and sustaining a commercial network, practically from scratch, in a territory where the British, French, and Russians had been operating for years.

But the purpose of the mission was obviously something altogether different, and that purpose was achieved: to snatch a first-class ticket in the assault on the world. After the defeat at Adua, there was a desperate need to restore national pride and reaffirm the will to sit as equals with the other "whites." From this point of view, the mission was a success. Nascent Italian public opinion was captivated by the Boxer Rebellion, and the valour of the Italian soldiers inspired the imagination of the times. Emilio Salgari would even write a fairly successful novel on the subject: *Le stragi della China* [The Massacres in China], also published under the title, *Il sotterraneo della morte* [The Dungeon of Death].[40]

The fact that Italy was once again made a tool of British colonialism—to replenish the ranks of the anti-Chinese expeditionary corps by stoking Italian ambitions—did not seem to trouble the government nor Italian public opinion. Having been at the concert of nations, and reading newspaper accounts of Italian envoys sitting elbow to elbow with British, French, and German envoys was more than enough of a return on Italy's investment in China.

The "Tianjin Concession" thus became part of Italy's overseas colonial domains. Life in the concession, which was little more than a multi-ethnic neighbourhood, would inspire sporadic, mostly stereotypical articles in Italian media over the next forty years. Almost forgotten diplomatically and non-existent commercially, "Italian" Tientsin remained an expensive display of imperial politics without any relevant influence in the panoply of Italian colonial culture. Maintained as little more than a curiosity—a luxury parking garage for diplomats—its claim to fame would be the first sighting of a young and reckless Galeazzo Ciano before he married Benito Mussolini's daughter Edda. But the concession would always carry out the task that it was assigned by Italian diplomacy since its inception: demonstrating Italy's right to the status of great power.

After a sleepy forty years, the Italian territory in China would be occupied by the Japanese during World War II, following Italy's surrender on September 8, 1943. The peace treaty of February 10, 1947, formalized the return of the concession to China and the loss of that small slice of overseas territory that had never really captured the Italian colonial imagination.

"Tripoli, the Fourth Shore"

While Eritrea, Somalia, and Tientsin were more or less random destinations, driven by emotions and propaganda, Italy's attraction to Tripoli was not.

Finally, long after the Unification of Italy in 1861, the new-born Kingdom of Italy had found a natural destination for its expansionist ambitions—the southern shore of the Mediterranean. For centuries, the North African coast had been an important commercial and social partner for the peninsula. Well before 1861, the Kingdom of Naples, the Republic of Venice, and even Piedmont had exercised a high degree of influence in the Mediterranean. For example, it was in Tripoli in 1825 that the navy of the then Kingdom of Sardinia made one of its rare demonstrations of strength. Savoy warships bombarded the port installations in retaliation against pirates who, at the time, were finding refuge in the city; an operation that the Sardinian kingdom repeated in 1833.[41]

In the nineteenth century, the Mediterranean continued to be a trading area rather than a border. On the south coast, in particular, many port cities were comprised of multicultural, multi-ethnic, and multi-religious communities— notions that were "pre-national," we might say, that is, not yet embedded in the logic of the linguistic, cultural, territorial, and historical context of nineteenth-century Europe.

Throughout the nineteenth century, trade opportunities and the relatively short distance from Europe favoured "white" immigration to North Africa. Tripoli itself hosted a sizeable Italian community, as did other coastal cities such as Alexandria and, especially, Tunis. In 1881, the Italian population in the Regency of Tunis was estimated at 11,000.[42] This garnered the attention of the new-fangled Italian desire for expansion; the city was right across the channel from Sicily; it had a stable and well-entrenched Italian presence (a district was even named "little Sicily"); and it offered very interesting economic prospects. Finally, twenty years after Unification, Italy had found on the Tunisian coast what it had been looking for.

For this reason, the declaration of a French protectorate over Tunisia, in 1881, was a shock for Italian diplomacy and a cold shower for public opinion. The bitter humiliation of the *fait accompli* was a mortal wound to the national interest. While the southern shore of the Mediterranean was not vital to the peninsula's economy at that time, many in Italy believed that Tunis would have been the first stage of an emergent Italian expansionism. As French troops crossed the border from Algeria into Tunisia, an Italian editorialist remarked:

> Tunis was our beachhead to the African continent. If one day the inner riches of this vast land will be accessible to Europe, it is through Tunis that they will flow, towards Italy. Tunis is our road to the heart of Africa. And this road is now closed to us.[43]

Above all, the snub was perceived as putting a stop to Italy's international expansionist aims, and it brought Italian politics face to face with its own international irrelevance. As had happened before, and as would happen time after time, the fire of Italian imperialism was fuelled by prestige and a badly concealed inferiority complex.

The problem with the North African coast in the second half of the nineteenth century, is that, unfortunately for the Italian government, it was already a very crowded "piece of the land." France controlled all the land from Morocco to

Tunis via Algeria, and Egypt was a British protectorate. The remaining stretch included two coastal regions which were under Turkish control—Tripolitania, namely, the region around Tripoli; and Cyrenaica, named after the ancient Roman city of Cyrene, whose capital was Benghazi.

Of the possible destinations, Tripoli seemed the most attractive in terms of size and possibilities. It was much less interesting than Tunis, but nevertheless within reach of the Italians, provided they could persuade the other powers.

Ottoman sovereignty over the city did not seem to bother Italian diplomacy. Constantinople's control over the territory was very scant. In fact, in both Tripolitania and Cyrenaica anti-Turkish sentiment had led to a series of revolts fuelled by independentist sentiments. One of the Italian government's strategies was precisely to play the role of "emancipator" from Ottoman rule with the local population. But Turkey was not the Italians' main concern: what really mattered was finding the right moment to begin the conquest without provoking negative reactions from the other colonial powers.

The biggest obstacle was Britain's rather frigid response to the idea. As with all other Italian colonial adventures, the Tripoline one needed British consent, or at least tacit approval. The problem was that the Mediterranean was not the Red Sea. While London was willing to accept a nominal Italian presence on the Indian Ocean, in the coastal town of Assab and near Zanzibar—desolate areas of little strategic or commercial value—it was quite another matter to allow the Mediterranean to be totally occupied by other Western powers. In the case of an arrangement between France and Italy, no matter how unlikely, together the two countries could counter the strategic weight of the British navy and potentially bar the British from the shortest route between Britain and India.

It was mostly for this reason that the Italian approach to Tripoli and the southern coast of the Mediterranean, unlike

Eritrea and Somalia, had a much longer incubation period. This also allowed the national press and public opinion to normalize the idea of an "Italian Tripoli." Ever since the French seized Tunis, there had been talk, especially in the press, of Tripoli as possible "compensation" for Italian claims, and of Tripolitania and Cyrenaica as zones of influence for Rome. Joining the Triple Alliance in defiance of the French, wearing down the international image of the Ottoman Empire, and bolstering its fleet at the risk of emptying the state's coffers were among the measures Italy took to fulfil its role as a great power in the Mediterranean. And, once again, it must do so to reaffirm its prestige. If Eritrea and Somalia were collateral diplomatic challenges, now at the turn of the century, Tripoli had become one of the cornerstones of Italy's foreign policy.[44]

The first decade of the twentieth century saw a turn of events that boded well for Italy's position: increased tension between France and Germany between 1905 and 1911[45] over what would go down in history as the "Moroccan crises"; the final phase of the Ottoman Empire's decline; and the swallowing up of Bosnia-Herzegovina in 1908, at the expense of the Turks, by Austria-Hungary (an alliance partner that Italy found difficult to digest, but who seemed to acquiesce to Italy's ambitions).[46]

Fifteen years after Adua and fifty years after Unification, the moment for the leap southwards seemed at hand, and liberal Italy seemed ready. Matters were accelerated by the difficulties within the government of Giovanni Giolitti, who chose to play the war card to re-organize his majority and divert attention from his failures. The Royal House of Savoy, as often happened in Italy's history, fervently supported what seemed an easy and glorious adventure. The military and industrial apparatus declared themselves ready for the challenge. A large segment of the country's economic and cultural elite seemed favourable to the venture.

On the other hand, public opinion took a less sanguine view. The nation was suffering from enormous social inequalities and internal deficiencies—an economic crisis with no end in sight. Hundreds of thousands of Italians were leaving the country permanently. The social issues exposed the systemic impasse in which liberal Italy found itself. The last thing the country needed was another colonial adventure whose costs would certainly be considerable and outcomes dubious. Fuelled by economic and humanitarian motivations, the country's pacifist movement started coming together, organizing demonstrations that sometimes led to street clashes.[47] Among the most fervent pacifists was a certain Benito Mussolini, then an ardent socialist, who was actually arrested on October 14, 1911, on charges of, among other things, "inciting violence, resisting the police, violating the freedom of recruits and shopkeepers, and damaging railway, telephone and telegraph lines."[48]

The image of Italy's existing colonies did not help the idea of new conquests. In 1911, Italy's overseas budget was woefully in the red: Eritrea and Somalia were using up considerable human and financial resources, and seemingly gave nothing in return. Despite a variety of development plans, the colonial governments' budgets remained appallingly in deficit, leaving nothing to build the necessary infrastructures that would allow the overseas economy to take off. On paper, at least, it seemed that the conquest of a tract of arid African land was not, in any way, the solution to any of Italy's problems. But ironically, this was exactly how the invasion was sold.

"The White Man Has a Right to the African Paradise"

In 1911, Italian newspapers introduced the Italian public to "Libya," an old geographic name, that encompassed the regions of Tripolitania, Cyrenaica, and Fezzan, and presented it as the panacea for all Italian ills. Libya was the name by which the colony would later be known.

The lands to be conquered, described as an agricultural paradise, would be the happy outlet for Italian emigrants—finally able to apply their genius to a land owned by their country. The overappraisal of Tripolitania and Cyrenaica's wealth was nothing less than ridiculous. The much-vaunted fertility of the soil was met with irony by those who opposed the enterprise. One of the more famous descriptions is attributed to the socialist Gaetano Salvemini, who depicted Libya as a "giant sandbox"—something that, over the years, the Italian occupiers themselves would recognize as rather accurate. Yet, the enterprise was presented as eminently advantageous from an agricultural point of view. Oddly, little was made of the commercial possibilities of the ports, which were already, for the most part, available to the Italians. But Libya was seen as being too close geographically to Italy. Development of its ports would be largely at the expense of Sicilian ports. Since the territory had no worthy domestic consumer market, it would at best be developed into a trading post. Besides, it was said that Libya's real wealth lay in the land.

The emphasis was effectively put on making the North African territory attractive to agricultural settlers. The basic belief was that the "Arabs" were too few in relation to the immensity of the territory, and, anyway, they did not know how to make the most of their own land. Therefore, this land should be put in the hands of those who knew how to make it prosper. In this case, as in others, the invaders did not have a clear idea of the complex society they were about to attack, seeing it as inhabited merely by an indistinct mass of people. At the very least, this typically racist and imperialist view had the advantage of avoiding the hypocritical rhetoric of the need to export civilization. The right to a fertile land, in spite of the fact that it was already inhabited, replaced the notion of trying to cloak colonialism as civilization, as had been done during the public discussions on Eritrea. By 1911, Italy had a "right," so to speak, over Libya, and therefore claimed it.

It was further argued that the military undertaking would bolster the Italian armaments industry and relaunch this sector of the economy. But above all, it was believed that the Libyan adventure would pay off immediately. The problems encountered in making Eritrea and Somalia profitable could be attributed to the distance from the metropolitan territory and the backwardness of the subjugated populations. In Libya there seemed to be far fewer difficulties. The distance between Italy's southern reaches and Libya's shores was a few short hours by sea, and the territory's coastal cities appeared much less foreign and more modern than the settlements on the Red Sea and the Indian Ocean. It was precisely this proximity that made public opinion perceive Libya as less "wild" than the previous conquests. It was not the "Black Africa" described in Joseph Conrad's novels, but a "southerly" neighbour out of *The Arabian Nights*. This was not a minor detail, as in the minds of many, to make Libya attractive to agricultural settlers, it had to be presented as an extension of Sicily and Southern Italy.

But critics of the venture would not be silenced, pointing out that it would be better to use the money on "civilizing" Italy itself, than blowing it on Libya. The opposition newspapers were quick to expose the flaws in the government's propaganda. The desire to civilize—supposedly one of the reasons for the attack on Libya—was mocked from many quarters. A commentator in the socialist daily, *Avanti!*, wrote:

> The Italian South, still barbarously African, can never hope to become civilly European, as long as the hundreds of millions, indispensable for its redemption and civilization in fact and not in platitudes, are squandered on dreaming, preaching and promoting the delinquent and anti-Italian conquests of Eritrea

and Benadir, and the conquests about to be perpetrated in the targeted parts of Tripolitania.[49]

The challenge brought forth by the socialists, and a smattering of anti-colonialist groups, had its own compelling logic, which, even before the age of international solidarity, pointed to the fact that there were economic and social reasons to reject the idea of creating an overseas empire. These dissonant voices, however, were in the minority and, above all, they underestimated the important role played by the media in promoting the enterprise, and the leverage the media had on public opinion. The considerations driving the stakes were decidedly emotional, not logical.

The Libyan War of 1911-12 was one of colonial aggression, though it was sold as a war of national redemption. Many of the most prominent intellectuals of the time took sides in favour of military intervention. The speech given by poet and classical scholar Giovanni Pascoli in November 1911, as the war was getting underway, is among the most infamous:

> The great Proletarian is in motion. First, she sent her labourers abroad, as there were too many at home and they had to work for too little... In America, they had become rather like the Negroes, these fellow countrymen of the man who discovered her; and like the Negroes they were sometimes put outside the law and humanity, and they were lynched... Blessed are ye who have died for the Fatherland! You do not know what you are to us and to History! You do not know what Italy owes you! Italy, now fifty years since its creation. On the sacred fiftieth anniversary, you have given proof of the vow made by our greats; they who never hoped it would be fulfilled so soon. You have shown that Italians, too, have proven themselves.[50]

In his speech, Pascoli succeeded in capturing the deep, emotional motives for the war. The words he chose were evocative and revealing, all the more so because they were from the man who was considered the greatest Italian poet of his time. At stake was not a simple colonial adventure. In

Tripoli, it was about proving oneself—to the whole world, but also to oneself.

With weapons in hand, the goal was to consecrate the notion that Italians were not like "Negroes in America." The emotional and racist component overtakes all the other motivations. Never mind the objections that are continuously raised about committing the fragile state budget to an enterprise that has such meagre prospects. Never mind that the idea of turning the territory around Tripoli into a settler colony is quite vague and scarcely feasible. A "self-respecting" world power must successfully participate in the "scramble for Africa," or lose its status.

Not least, Libya was a test-case for the ideology of biological supremacy that proliferated in Italy and in the rest of Europe: to conquer Africa was to dispel any doubt that one was rightfully part of that world of conquering "whites" praised by Kipling. Tripoli was also reparations for Adua.

Italy's powerbrokers were thus carrying the white man's burden and, no matter the cost, making him the symbol of those who belong at the top of the world. This attitude would soon descend into colonial racism and give a funereal accent to all of Italy's policies in Africa throughout the twentieth century.

Pacify at Any Cost

The conquest and administration of Tripolitania and Cyrenaica encapsulated all the difficulties and contradictions of Italian colonialism, as it had in the Horn of Africa and as it would later during the Fascist regime. After an easy victory over the Ottoman troops in the coastal cities, to their surprise the Italians were met with resistance from the many local tribes. This resistance would be long and fierce, and it would be suppressed in blood. What was sold as a quick military victory turned into one of the longest conflicts the Italian military would face.[51]

Figure 1: Colonial Libya

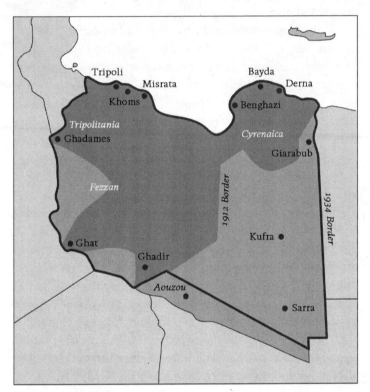

Many Italians were deluded into thinking they could present themselves to the populations of the conquered lands as liberators. But after an initial positive reception, a series of miscalculations by the Italians antagonized virtually all the local powers. In addition, a handful of Turkish officers had stayed behind and managed to unite the many factions in Tripoline and Cyrenaica around a shared religious cause, thus launching a guerrilla war. Very quickly, the Italians' triumphal march was met by a holy war against the infidels. The lack of knowledge and the underestimation of the conquered are usually the principal causes of the difficulties encountered by invaders. Although the Libyan adventure was by far the best planned and organized up to that time, the invaders showed little knowledge and understanding of the local dynamics.

Giolitti hastened to proclaim Italy's conquest—the first Italian troops landed in Tripoli on October 3, 1911, and the decree of annexation was signed by the king on November 5,[52] making the invasion a real lightning war. But the conflict dragged on, and a series of clashes quickly shattered the idea that the new lands could immediately be transformed into the promised paradise.

The unexpected resistance to the invasion unequivocally exposed Italy's propaganda of a land that was a ripened fruit ready to be picked. As things did not go as planned, the Italian military unleashed a blind, animalistic fury. At the end of October 1911, a series of bloody uprisings on the outskirts of Tripoli were brutally repressed by the occupying troops. "The city was put to the sword: perhaps 1800 people in Tripoli in a population of 30,000 were shot or hanged in an act of reprisal."[53]

Never imagining that the occupied would even contemplate resistance and, above all, with the ill-concealed sentiment that they were dealing with non-Europeans and, therefore, with people not entitled to human dignity, the Italians let themselves go—destroying, looting, raping, and ravaging—with an intensity that would have been unthinkable in a European conflict.

The disproportionate use of violence is one of the most damaging aspects of imperialist racism, and the events in Tripoli showed how, although the Italian colonial Empire was not equal to the other white powers, the savagery with which the Italians built it was second to none.

What hovered over everything was the dread that Italy would make a bad international impression. The Italian-Turkish war was a test of maturity for liberal Italy—the umpteenth one—that the country could not afford to fail. This was a widely shared notion, given the Italian media's own battle to counter the news of Italy's defeats reported in the international press. For example, in the pages of *Corriere della Sera*, journalist and politician Andrea Torre (1866-1940) complained:

> Much of the Austrian and German press continues to give erroneous and even false news of the war in Tripolitania, and it continues to be driven by an unjustifiable malice towards us. It is ridiculous that they would deem the preposterous and inconclusive news coming from Constantinople as serious and truthful. Meanwhile, they disregard the precise and reliable news given by the official communiqués of the Italian government and the most trustworthy press services in our country.[54]

Torre's remarks highlighted Italians' inability to accept that otherwise "friendly newspapers" and fellow members of the Triple Alliance would put Italians and Turks on the same level. He even goes so far as to float the idea of an international conspiracy to justify this apparent about-turn:

> It is interesting to note that most of the press that is defending the uncivilized Turks over civilized Italians is inspired by a certain cosmopolitan financial element whose interests would be harmed by our current action, and more so in the event of the collapse of the Ottoman Empire.[55]

There were concerns of a possible betrayal by international finance because, in fact, it was incomprehensible that Europeans should give more credit to the Turks than to whites. The vehemence of the attack in these and other editorials suggested an increasing sense of unease, even fear. It was a fear Italians had already experienced, in Adua in 1896; a fear of failure that had humiliated the country and had relegated it to the fringes of the club of white imperial powers.

The guerrilla war dragged on for decades, with continuous ups and downs, except for a hiatus imposed by World War I, when Libyan affairs took a back seat, both in the priorities of the government and in the collective imagination. Gradually, the idea of the Libyan paradise gave way to yet another expression of the colony as a wild and inhospitable land, only useful for fictional adventures and illegal trafficking.

After World War I, the work of subjugation, now blatantly defined as the "reconquest" of the rebellious colony, gained new momentum. A new governor, Giuseppe Volpi (1877-1947) arrived in Tripoli in 1921. What took place under his leadership was a systematic military occupation of the territory. This drive received further impetus with the coming to power of Benito Mussolini. The Fascist regime continued the policies and aims of the preceding liberal governments of subjugating the local population through violence. The reconquest of Libya took on even more propaganda value after 1922, as the regime interpreted the resistance of the turbulent colony as a direct affront to its own ability to manage the territory. Where the weak liberal democracy had failed, the new regime would triumph. To do so, it did not skimp on resources and violence.

In 1929, Rodolfo Graziani led the last phase of the repression.[56] Through a painstaking and extremely costly military occupation, he took control of the entire coastline. He pushed inland into the region of Fezzan. Here, the Italian army employed the fiercest counter-guerrilla techniques: bombing civilian populations, using poison gas, and deporting civilians to concentration camps[57] to deprive the Libyan partisans of any form of support. Such a methodical annihilation of people led some historians to raise the spectre of genocide.[58] With the capture of resistance leader Omar al-Mukhtar in 1931, twenty years after the start of the invasion, Italy's grand operations in Libya came to an end, and the colony was declared "pacified." The human cost for the local population was severe. Deportations, massacres, and destruction complemented the triumph of "Pax Italiana." Through it, the Mussolini regime conveyed a very clear message to the Italian masses: the only thing that colonial populations understood was the most heinous and inhuman violence.

At the end of the campaign, Rodolfo Graziani was rewarded with a nickname that gave the full measure of homegrown Italian colonialism—"Butcher of Fezzan,"[59] a macabre nickname that he did not repudiate.

A twenty-year period of open war (1911-1931) and another full decade of more or less passive resistance (1931-1942) left deep scars in the way the local populations saw themselves. Tripolitania, Cyrenaica, and Fezzan would together gain independence in 1950 under the name "United Kingdom of Libya." The greatest colonial legacy was indeed the fact that the different peoples and regions that made up the former Italian possession were united in the common fight against the invader, and became a nation.

The Dodecanese, a Strange "White" Colony

The war against the Ottoman Empire in 1911-12 also gave Italy possession of the Dodecanese, a group of islands in the Aegean, the largest of which is Rhodes.[60] Strategically located on the route between the Mediterranean and the Black Sea, the islands were occupied by the Italian Navy during the Libyan War to pressure the Turks into accepting the terms of surrender.

The signing of a peace treaty in Lausanne between Italy and Turkey, on October 18, 1912, provided for the withdrawal of the Italian occupation troops from the islands. However, this was never carried out, as the Italians claimed that Turkey continued to foment resistance in Libya after the war. The Italian government administered the islands illegally from 1912 until February 4, 1923, when a second Treaty of Lausanne recognized Italy's de facto possession of the islands.

The life of this "anomalous" colony in the panorama of Italian imperialism was marked above all by the play of international politics. Given their strategic location, the islands were kept under direct military administration for a decade. The first civilian governor, Mario Lago (1878-1950), only took office on November 16, 1922. With the Fascists' rise to power, the islands acquired new value: a showcase for Italian imperialism. Some urban infrastructure works were started, especially on the main island of Rhodes; and some commercial ventures were attempted that tried to induce Italian immigration to the archipelago, but these remained very sporadic.

The idea, extolled by the propaganda, was that the Dodecanese was the "gateway to the Levant," the eastern extension of Italy's Mediterranean expansionist aims. Thus, a policy was fashioned to reaffirm the Italian character of the islands. Its ancient ties with its Venetian past were dusted off, emphasizing their possession as the rightful inheritance of the Serenissima. Immigration was strongly encouraged, but it was presented as a "resettlement" in lands that were already Italian. Despite the regime's efforts, the 1936 census, the last before World War II, recorded just 7000 Italians out of a population of almost 130,000, mostly concentrated in Rhodes.[61]

However, other than using the occupation as a propaganda tool, it was immediately clear that the Dodecanese was not, nor could it be, a colony like any other. Already, during the first days of the military occupation, the idea, for example, of having a two-tier judicial system—one for locals and one for occupiers like in Eritrea—was discarded. As "whites," the inhabitants of the islands, whether Greek or Turk, could not be subjected to an apartheid regime as it was being applied in the African colonies, or even in neighbouring Libya. During the first occupation period, when the colony was still administered by the military, Italian officials even agreed to let the locals continue to use Ottoman customs and regulations, suggesting that the occupation could still be temporary. This notion was further reinforced by the fact that during and immediately following World War I, the islands in question were claimed more than once by Athens. A secret agreement between Greece and Italy[62] suggested as much: the Dodecanese would be handed over to Greece in return for Greece's support of Italy's claims on Albania.

It was only in the 1920s, once their possession was confirmed, that the islands were identified as a possible beachhead for "Italianization," and that the first serious attempts were made to bring the Aegean into the fold of Italian imperialism. This was a rather peculiar position for Italy to be in, compared to the other areas it occupied, as it was clear that the islands could not be much more than a costly display of Italian success. As Francesco Dessy, an official responsible for the agricultural development of the Aegean colony, wrote in 1933:

> Italy, beleaguered by the need to find land overseas for the production of raw materials and space for its expanding population, can receive neither one nor the other from its tiny Aegean possession. However, its role there is just as useful for the national interest as it is in the colonies. Indeed, being in contact with peoples who have reached a degree of civilization similar to our own, Italy is called upon to demonstrate the maturity to assume the role of leader in every field—a sort of test for others to see. We must awaken new subjects from their weariness, like the foreigners in neighbouring lands who have taken on the same task as we have. This is the mission that Italy is called upon to fulfil in the East, where the memories of its glory and greatness are perpetuated and revived.[63]

The theme of civilization in this sense is more effectively invoked than any other to justify the determination to dominate. That is, the occupation would be used to show the way to peoples who are just a little behind in the race toward civilization, presenting the Italian variety as more mature and suitable to unveil the latest advancements in civilization to the inhabitants of the Aegean, who are white but not yet fully "adult."

This was the main reason for the peculiar situation in the Dodecanese. Unlike other territories, it was never formally declared a "colony." Such a legal definition was discarded during the first ten years of occupation and replaced in the official record with the more vague "Italian territory."

From 1924, during the centralizing drive of the Fascist regime, the term "possession" began to be used. What meaning this expression has from a legal point of view is not any clearer. But at the very least it detached the Aegean islands, in practical and semantic terms, from the context of "Italian colonies."

There was a structural difficulty in trying to define this territory, as it did not present the classical characteristics of a colony. Above all, on an ideological level, the fact is that it was not populated by "clearly inferior" people, namely blacks. For the Italians—the public as well as the rulers—colonies are places where "inferior races" live, not whites.

The issue of how to situate the Aegean peoples in the context of Italian rule was one on which Fascist legal minds were most diligently engaged. They were aided in this endeavour by the pseudo-scientific positions of the regime's scientists, who in the 1930s ascertained the racial non-inferiority of the indigenous Greeks.[64] Thus, their status lay somewhere between full Italian citizen and colonial subject. This allowed the inhabitants of the Dodecanese the right to apply for full Italian citizenship during the Fascist regime.[65] This was not the case for any of the other Italian colonies.

The absence of this thirty-year Mediterranean domination in the collective memory of Italians lies precisely in its eccentricity with respect to the "model." In this "colony/non-colony," Italian imperialism demonstrated the full extent—the very nature, one might say—of the racist colonial ideology. It was not a question of territory, but of race. Nor was it a question of distance from the centre of power or remoteness in terms of civilization, real or imagined. Colonies are places where the whites meet individuals who are diverse, black, submissive—to educate them or, more often, to exploit them.

"Abyssinia: The Fascist Empire"

All knots have been undone by our shimmering sword, and the African victory has become part of the history of the Fatherland, whole and pure, like the fallen and surviving legionnaires dreamt it and wished it. Italy finally has its empire, a Fascist Empire, because it bears the indestructible signs of the will and power of the Roman lictor, because this was the goal towards which the bursting and disciplined energies of the young and gallant Italian generations have been driven to for fourteen years. It is an Empire of Peace because Italy wants peace, for itself and for all, and only decides for war when it is forced into it by the imperious, incoercible necessities of life. It is an Empire of Civilization and Humanity, for all the peoples of Ethiopia... The Italian people created the Empire with their blood. They will fertilize it with their labour, and defend it against anyone with their arms. In this supreme certainty, raise your insignia, your iron, your hearts, and salute, O Legionaries, after fifteen centuries, the reappearance of the empire on the fated hills of Rome. Will you be worthy of it? (the crowd shouts "Yes!") This cry is like a sacred oath, binding you before God and before men, for life and for death! Black shirts, legionaries, Hail the King! (Transcript of the recording of Mussolini's speech proclaiming the Empire, May 9, 1936.)[66]

Unlike other Italian colonial invasions, the act of aggression against Ethiopia in 1935 has been the subject of numerous interpretations and analyses, and has left a much stronger impression on the public memory and the conscience of Italians.

This is due to the determination with which this aggression was recounted and promoted. The Ethiopia of 1935 was a "Fascist" enterprise. Indeed, we can call it "the Fascist enterprise par excellence"—more so than the intervention in Spain, where the stage was more often occupied by other actors, namely the Soviet Union and Nazi Germany; more so than the Fascist War of 1940 itself, where the role of the Mussolini regime as a supporting actor compared to its German ally was immediately evident.

Ethiopia in 1935, on the other hand, was more than any other, a "made in Italy" feat of totalitarianism—both in the way it unfolded and, above all, in the way it was recounted to and received by the population at the time and by subsequent generations. And it was, more clearly than others, a "victorious war"[67] or, at least, perceived as such.

All the rhetorical ruses previously deployed for other overseas adventures were used in the propaganda regarding the Ethiopian Empire in the 1930s: the dream of fabulous riches to be exploited; the creation of an outlet for emigration; the need to carry on the dream of civilizing backward peoples.[68]

But what actually distinguished the propaganda regarding Ethiopia from that of Eritrea, Somalia, and even Libya was the value of the conquest as an "epochal challenge." The elements of this challenge, crystallized in the Italian public narrative of the time, were very clear. First among these was the fabricated challenge of the "new Italy" against the old western demo-plutocracies, and Great Britain in particular whom, as we saw, was until then the true arbiter of the destinies of Italian imperialism. Mussolini's colonialism wanted to present itself as "mature" and independent. In a strange sort of unresolved Oedipal complex, it was precisely against the British Empire that Fascist propaganda was aimed during the assault on Abyssinia.[69]

The conquest was also sold as a battle of the "young" nations against the old, in a Darwinian struggle for survival that would be put forth anew by the regime when Italy

Figure 2: The Italian Empire during the Fascist Regime

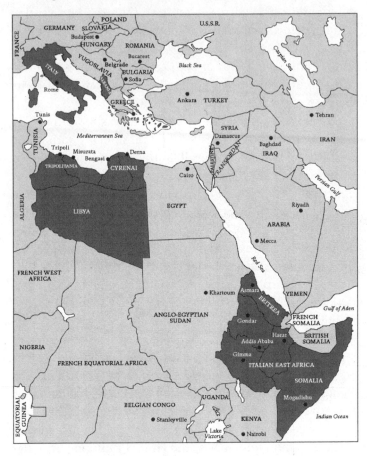

entered World War II alongside Hitler's Germany.[70] This reading is fundamental because it detached, for the benefit of Italian public opinion, the prestige of the conquest from its actual economic utility.

In addition, the conquest of Ethiopia had been brandished by the Fascist regime for some time as a goal by which Italy's greatness could be measured—a goal the former Italian liberal establishment of the late-nineteenth and early-twentieth centuries had failed to achieve. Manipulated over many years by Fascist propaganda, the Italian masses normalized the notion that Italy was entitled to that slice of Africa and that confrontation was inevitable. From the start, Mussolini presented himself as the fulfilment of liberal Italy's unkept promises, and the "Ethiopian question" was no exception. In presenting himself as the possible "Avenger of Adua,"[71] the Duce cleverly played his hand.

For Eritrea, Somalia, and Libya it had been necessary to construct a "utilitarian" narrative, at least in the beginning—these were valuable lands, necessary for the country's development. When the exaggerated hopes were dashed, many commentators articulated the bitterness of getting stuck with useless and costly colonies, thus fomenting a sense of disillusionment with imperialism itself. But Ethiopia was different: it was extolled as a treasure trove to be exploited from the very first attempts at conquest in the late nineteenth century. In Mussolini's speeches it further took the form of a "maturity test" of Fascist imperialism. The usefulness of the conquest was to be measured, above all, by its returns, namely prestige. Once the test was passed, with the seizure of Addis Ababa, everyone moved quickly to enshrine the achievement with the much-coveted title: Italy had its empire. After more than fifty years of trying, the country seemed to have earned the right to be a member of the club of great powers.

The new title assumed by Victor Emmanuel III, of king and emperor, mimics that of the English monarch as sovereign of the United Kingdom and emperor of the Indian Raj—a formal parity that the Italian regime, as well as the court and the House of Savoy, did not fail to emphasize.

The invasion of Ethiopia became a re-enactment of the great battles for Unification or the Great War, rather than an act of imperialist expansion. The supercharged rhetoric—that peoples must face historical "trials" to conquer their place in human history—had the desired effect. All that remained was for the regime to reap the benefits of the unity of the masses in support of the enterprise.

Only a few free anti-Fascists remained (as most were in jail or in exile) to bemoan the fact that this was a war of aggression launched against a sovereign state, which sat in the League of Nations. In any case, these arguments were not resonating with Italian society. Firstly, Fascist censorship and repression prevented their dissemination; secondly, the message of a riposte against the other white powers was too strong. The paradox lay precisely in the fact that the invasion of Ethiopia was largely presented as a war of liberation from the hegemony of European nations that arose from the Treaty of Versailles of 1919.[72]

The feeling of retribution had overtaken the country long before the "mutilated victory" in the War of 1915-18. Italian Ethiopia was compensation for seventy-five years of disappointments, frustrated ambitions, and real or presumed humiliations in the international arena. Nothing could be done to counter this narrative, especially once Addis Ababa was conquered and the fruits of the conquest could be reaped—and despite the counter-narratives that spoke of injustices, violence, and massacres of free peoples, not to mention the exorbitant costs in terms of human and other resources. The imperial title, which Ethiopia brought as a dowry, could justify any outrage.

As we shall see, Fascist propaganda obviously described the adversary in the most blatantly racist terms. The territory of Abyssinia itself was recounted as ferocious and beastly, which in the typical European imagination recalled all the stereotypes of "black" Africa. Thus, it should come as no surprise that public opinion raised no objections to waging war, even though it was against a free and sovereign state. In addition, as nothing more than beasts, the inhabitants of the Ethiopian Empire were a disgrace to the League of Nations.

The presence of such a barbaric and backward state in the international forum proved that the forum itself was a hoax, a trap, set by imperialist nations to maintain the status quo and prevent others from gaining a place among the dominant peoples.

This emotional investment, interwoven with the very fate of Italy as a nation, gave rise to a series of consequences, some very severe, in the way the conquest was conducted and how authority was established. Contempt for an enemy considered eminently subhuman greatly amplified the brutality employed in battle, justified the use of poison gas and systematic violence against civilians, and gave rise to an apartheid regime and the implementation of racist legislation.[73] The fear of a military failure, in what was perceived as the supreme challenge, resulted in the use of massive resources: the deployment of hundreds of thousands of men and the most advanced technology of the day in the form of planes, tanks, and mechanized wagon trains—unthinkable before then for a colonial enterprise.[74] The costs were so onerous that they undermined the country's military capacity—a crisis from which Italy had not yet recovered by 1939, when war broke out in Europe.[75] The determination to establish dominance and the fear of demonstrating weakness in the international arena, especially in the early days after the invasion, led to the creation of a veritable reign of terror, which would remain in place in many parts of the conquered empire until liberation in 1941.

Many historians have highlighted the fact that Italy's Ethiopian enterprise was the last great conquest by an imperialism rooted in the second half of the nineteenth century, whose impetus was now out of step with how colonialism was evolving. Already, in 1931, with the Statute of Westminster, Britain was seeking to transform its colonial position by recognizing "dominions"—colonies with a sizable white presence. This "investment" would be pivotal for the apprehended war in Europe. Meanwhile, the Fascist regime was moving backwards. Economically fruitless, internationally detrimental, and fleeting (exactly five years from the time Italian troops entered Addis Ababa, on May 5, 1936, to when the Negus Haile Selassie returned to the capital, on May 5, 1941), the invasion of Ethiopia is nevertheless, and by far, the colonial event that most marked the historical consciousness of Italians. And, as we shall see, it is the one that most influenced the (mis)understanding of Africa by the Italy's civil society.

Chapter 3

Contacts

Prejudice from Overseas

Once upon a time there was the Negus
And now he is no more
Once a merry festoon
Who thought he was the great Solomon
After serving coffee
He had the *chitet* cut down
We want an outlet to the sea
To be able to wash now and then
He said this as he loaded his parasol
And climbed on his donkey.
O Negus, o Negus
What calamity awaits you.

Fernando Crivelli (Crivel)
"Once Upon a Time There Was the Negus" (song, 1936)

Now that we have described the mechanisms that supported or, at least, did not hinder the march of Italian colonial imperialism, it would seem fitting to discuss the public narrative around the colonies and their inhabitants during the occupation.

Who can best describe for Italians the situation in the newly conquered lands, and by what means? The appearance and awareness of the workings of a culture that was quite different from the one Italy wanted to import unleashed very peculiar reactions and narratives, and marked how nascent Italian public opinion understood the overseas territories. These are reactions and narratives that persist to the present day.

The Rush to Conquer

When describing the phenomenon of Italian colonialism, for the sake of brevity, one often resorts to a rather peremptory statement: the Italians were the last ones in the "Scramble for Africa" and sought to occupy territories that were still free, that is, not already occupied by established colonial powers.

Although this definition succeeds in outlining rather precisely some of the destinations of made-in-Italy imperialist expansionism, it also reveals a misunderstanding of the situation in the territories that were gradually being conquered. While it is true that Italy invaded areas that were not subject to European domination, this does not mean that there were no forms of government there prior to the invasion.

In the public narrative that took root in the second half of the nineteenth century, the widespread idea was that "white government" was the only conceivable form of government. This is why many people believed that colonialism, and more so the Italian version, was exporting "civilization," in the broadest sense, to places where a more or less defined "state of nature" prevailed. The mission was perceived as not just worthy, but actually welcome—as a propaganda piece from 1892 explained:

> Our influence in Africa expands peacefully by the mere fact of our intellectual and moral superiority, and thanks to our abilities. Achieving this civilizing mission is the only thing that can legitimize Europe's conquests in Africa. There, we no longer have enemies. The tribes close to our possessions fall one after another into our sphere of influence out of empathy,

out of interest—we would almost say, by force of gravity—and our friendship is sought by the more distant tribes.[1]

A few years later, these assertions would have to reckon with the debacle at Adua.

This conception, the export of civilization as a real "mission," bordering on the religious, was one of the pillars of colonialism. Unfortunately, it continues as one of its posthumous justifications to this day. Moreover, for years the idea of dealing with "savages" was largely used as a justification to explain even the massive failures of Italian colonialism, and sway Italian public opinion. From Somalia to Libya and from Eritrea to Ethiopia, crises, clashes and the responsibility for violence were most often attributed to the "natives," who refused to understand how much good the white man was bringing. By foolishly rebelling, they unleashed the "just punishment" of the dominator. Yet, it is precisely in the Italian model that this would-be axiom proved far from realistic. In almost every case, the opposite was true—in the panoply of Italy's shoddy assaults on the lands belonging to others, one of the most complex operations was that of rooting out civilization in order to bring civilization.

Why Are We Here? I: We Are Occupying "Nobody's Land" (*Terra nullius*)

As we have seen, Italy's first action in its assault on territories to civilize was actually a trade deal.

> On this Monday, 11th day of the month of Shaban in the year 1286, according to the Islamic calendar, and the 15th day of the month of November in the year 1869, according to the European era, brothers Hassan-ben-Ahmad and Ibrahim-ben-Ahmad, and Mr Giuseppe Sapeto, being on board the Nasser-Megid, the boat belonging to Said-Auadh and having confirmed their presence, stipulated the following in the presence of witnesses: 1. The above-named brothers Hassan-ben-

Ahmad and Ibrahim-ben-Ahmad, Sultans of Assab, "sold and do sell to a Mr Giuseppe Sapeto the territory between Mount Ganga, Cape Lumah and the two sides thereof; wherefore, the dominion of the said territory shall belong to Mr Giuseppe Sapeto, as soon as he shall have disbursed the price thereof, they having freely sold it to him, voluntarily and with righteous intention.[2]

This was clearly a deed of sale, with all the formalities recognized at the time—and as they would be, more or less, even today. However, it seemed to raise issues of interpretation for the colonial vulgate: Was there sufficient knowledge on the part of the local population on the Red Sea in 1869 to be able to draft such a contract? Evidently, yes. And who would have enforced this contract? Evidently, the local justice system was sufficiently developed to be referenced in real estate transactions, even between local rulers and a private citizen.

If we look closely at this deed of sale, we can see that it implies a series of formal steps that should have altered the very perception of the colonial enterprise. The transaction was not a new reiteration of ancient relations between colonized and colonizers, as was reported mainly in the propaganda of the time or in the accounts of contemporaneous explorers. The purchase of Assab Bay was not comparable to the semi-mythical account of Peter Minuit's purchase of Manhattan, from the locals in 1626, for some beads and other trinkets—a gesture of cultural imposition that became the very symbol of the alleged naiveté and pliability of the conquered.

Assab was a private sale that shows how, in places preyed upon by the "explorers" of those times, there was, in fact, no unknown land to civilize: there was simply another civilization—a civilization that had been regulating everyday affairs according to its own code of law for centuries. They had institutions and laws that could not be arbitrarily bypassed—at least no more than they could be in Europe—but rather had to be respected in form and content.

It is interesting to note that, in the deed, the date of the Islamic calendar appears first, even in the Rubattino company's Italian translation. This clearly suggests that it is a product of local regulations. The fact that one of the contracting parties was a foreigner made it necessary to synchronize the calendars. Sapeto's is called the "European calendar," thereby invoking the modern notion of "multilateralism." The sultans of Assab recognized the existence of the European calendar but, of course, they did not perceive it as dominant.[3]

The acceptance of the binding nature of this contract, first by Sapeto and Rubattino and then by the Kingdom of Italy itself—which even published it in the Official Gazette as a historical antecedent to justify its colonial possession—constituted recognition of the actual sovereignty of the brother sultans over that little piece of land between sea and desert, and therefore also of their right to sell it. If anything, it was the Italian government that defied the laws of the sultanate—as well as those in Italy—and transformed a simple act of sale into a cession of sovereignty. Imagine if a foreign citizen bought a piece of land in Italy, turned it over to the government of his home country, and that government then declared that land as its sovereign possession. This would surely be considered an "uncivilized" act.

The purchase of Assab and its manipulation lead us to two conclusions: the Italian government, and all the other European powers taking part in the assault on Africa at the time, were well aware that the lands they were occupying were not previously ungoverned; they were not "empty" lands to be civilized. The manipulation of the Assab contract of 1869 presupposed the recognition of some kind of value to the contract and its issuer, even if it was only a recognition with the intention of justifying a misappropriation.[4] These were lands that had developed other forms of administration, sophisticated to the point of being able to reply in point of law to Italian claims at the international level, and which yielded their autonomy only through the explicit use of force.

But at home it was better to say that a new civilization was being built from scratch than say that an existing social system was being uprooted and replaced with colonial rule.

The notion that Italy was wading into an age-old primitivism was indeed widespread. It was confronted by indigenous peoples stuck in the Stone Age, who were completely unaware that they were wasting the riches of their land—riches that the law of white civilization bestowed, as it happened, to the whites themselves. This, it can be argued, was the underlying principle of all colonialism, whose pursuit was economic profit. Thanks to the technological revolution that began in the fifteenth century, Europeans are motivated to expand beyond their frontiers. They are driven so by numerous factors, but economics is the main one. As the historian Carlo M. Cipolla recalls, "when they began their long and perilous trek, the Europeans dreamed more of gold than of lost souls to bring out of the darkness."[5] However, it was definitely more useful to continue to imagine and describe the places to be conquered as devoid of any form of civilization.

Just like Assab and the shores of the Red Sea—where the agreements were made with Great Britain as the reigning colonial power and with local sultans whose independence was thwarted only through the use of force—the seemingly desolate Somali coast was no less devoid of autonomous governments. The sultans of Migiurtinia and Hobyo were very efficient administrators of their respective territories on the Indian Ocean. Both were the most recent heirs in a nearly uninterrupted sequence of governments, which began in the Horn of Africa, with the founding of Islam in the seventh century.

The agreements signed with the Italians were perceived by the local rulers not as an abdication of sovereignty but as an insurance policy and an international alliance to help maintain an internal equilibrium. The Italians themselves were seen as representatives of an external power that allowed them access to global spheres, but which left them relatively free in domestic affairs. As already mentioned, Italy actually paid the local sultans for accepting the protectorate, and did so until 1923, at which time the newly-established Fascist regime dismantled the local government structures[6] by force.[7] Until then, the relationship between colonizers and colonized was a contractual one, at least from the perspective of the Somalis. Here again, it was only with more advanced technology that the main structures of an ancient and articulate society could be violently swept away.

While local governments were being dismantled, throughout the colonial period Italian newspapers printed reports that painted the populations with a primitive aura, especially if the facts could be made to highlight the superiority of Italian civilization.

> Honour to Italy for intervening in the pitiful episode in Saati (Ethiopia). An Abyssinian slave girl, who had escaped from Ailet, appeared some days ago before the commander of the camp, asking for freedom and protection. Perhaps colonial policy demanded the return of the wretched girl to her owner; the latter probably demanded it from the Italian military authorities. However, whatever one may think of the intentions of the military command, let there be no doubt that once again civility was victorious over policy. Slavery still exists in Abyssinia, albeit more covertly than in the past.[8]

The episode in question as recounted in 1888 in the *Corriera della Sera* is an early example of a hagiographic trend in Western media in general, and in the Italian press in particular, which persists to this day[9]—that "white heroism" is a very useful tool to illustrate that intervention with the aim of "civilizing" is justified. Describing military interventions by dressing them up as the export of civilization was not enough for readers and, more generally, for public opinion to internalize the desired objective. But accompanying the accounts of clashes or reports of expropriations with news about the kindliness of Italians in general, and of Italian soldiers in particular, had a more immediate positive impact on the perception of the colonial effort. The Italians were in Africa to save the Abyssinian slaves. And to accomplish this, Italian soldiers were willing, even forced, to invoke realpolitik—violating political norms to assert the Royal Army's principle of defending the weak. They refused to turn over the slave girl, though she was never actually identified. She was simply described as a wretch (*disgraziata*). Nothing further about the poor wretch or her fate was reported. This is not surprising, since she was not the main character; the central figure in the story is, in fact, the army and its civilizing function through the use of force.

Why Are We Here? II: "We Are Modernity Against the Middle Ages"

A certain myopia concerning the history of the non-white peoples of Eritrea and Somalia was needed to support the propaganda that described the colonies as lands populated by savages. For these first two overseas occupations, silence and ignorance about the conditions of those territories before the arrival of the colonizers fuelled doubts that local forms of self-government could guarantee supposed standards of civilization. Fledgling public opinion could easily be told that the invaded lands belonged to no one, also because before the last quarter of the nineteenth century very few in Italy had even heard of the Sultans of Assab or the Sultans of Hobyo and Migiurtinia. However, a different narrative had to be created for the subsequent steps of Italian imperialism.

It was impossible to invoke the notion of a no man's land with respect to China. A civilization that was thousands of years old—whose technology had dominated the planet for centuries, and whose state apparatus had demonstrated extraordinary continuity—could not be branded as primitive. When the Kingdom of Italy took part in the expedition against the Boxers, it was barely forty years old; the Chinese Empire was about 4000.[10] Therefore, the paradigm had to be inverted: the decaying structures and their resistance to change over the centuries were China's real problems.

An atrophied country, stuck in the Middle Ages, corrupt and above all "decadent"; this was the narrative disseminated by the imperialist powers regarding non-European realities with a long history. While recognizing that certain peoples had achieved an evident degree of civilization, they had exhausted themselves, and progress required a change of pace, even if this implied a military shock.

Hence, the Italian expedition to China had the same civilizing value as the one on the shores of the Red Sea: building or rebuilding a civilization were among the task that "whites" needed to undertake. As in previous cases, news from the Chinese front was accompanied by accounts of massacres and violence—which confirmed the barbarity of the invaded—and by allegations of the Chinese government's inability to control the situation because of its weakness and corruption.

The image of a stagnant civilization, prevented for centuries from getting onto the road of progress, was equally applied to Tripolitania and Cyrenaica, while they were still officially part of the Ottoman empire. In popular bulletins and in the mainstream press, as well as in European chancelleries, Turkey was described as the "Sick man of Europe"[11]— an expression that conveyed a rotting structure that was gradually losing the characteristics that defined it as a modern state. In the eyes of the Italian government, the war with Turkey was also necessary to expel an inept and hopeless administration from a territory that would otherwise flourish in Italian hands. This is a rather unfortunate image, come to think of it, as it evokes jackals despoiling corpses. But presented in a positive light, it captured the imagination of people in 1911.

This is also why mass protests in cities like Tripoli or Benghazi, after the arrival of the soldiers of the Royal Italian Army, astonished and outraged so many: How can the "Libyans" not understand and appreciate the efforts being made to replace the old Turkish apparatus with the more modern and efficient (at least in theory) Italian system? This bewilderment, understood as a renunciation of civilization, unleashed a blind rage that led to brutal massacres of civilians. Being so backward as to reject civilization, the Libyans could therefore be punished with a degree of severity that would never be applied to civilized peoples. The perceived inferiority of the colonized was once again used to justify the use of beastly violence.

In the 1930s, Italy's propaganda against the Ethiopian Empire was a "cleverly sinister" blend of denying the very existence of civilization in those lands and the desire to conquer that very civilization because it was "stuck in the Middle Ages." The Empire was simultaneously described as wild, decadent, sick, and needing to be replaced so it could be brought into modernity, even by force, if necessary. The absence of a modern value system was highlighted in newspaper articles and newsreels. Much was made of different legal forms of servitude—which were systematically mispresented as slavery—and the corruption of the imperial establishment. Because of his short stature, Emperor Haile Selassie[12] became the subject of sarcastic jokes, and he was caricatured as having the classic attributes of the savage. But here too, the attempts at ridicule were bitterly ironic, given the well-documented short stature of Italy's King Victor Emmanuel III, who was, himself, the subject of brutal satirical jokes throughout his reign, both at home and abroad.

Despite an incongruent rhetoric, Italy managed to paint the Ethiopian Empire as both devoid of civilization, and as a civilization in its death throes. Either description—based on the non-understanding and non-acceptance of the Other—was reason enough to drive Italian colonial expansion. This non-acceptance was dramatically illustrated by the continuous dehumanization of the conquered, painting them as irreconcilably diverse. Being diverse from the conquerors is what condemns the colonized to their fate, and this diversity was constantly echoed by the propaganda.

Repeating the Stereotype to Reinforce Prejudice

This just in from Genoa:

> Yesterday [June 27, 1884] four natives with two children arrived from the Italian colony of Assab Bay. They are on their way to Turin, where tents were prepared for them within the Exhibition. The natives belong to the Dankali tribe. One, Ibrahim is the sultan's son and heir to the throne. He is 16 years old, and perfectly black. He wears a red *lorica* under a white silk mantle that goes down to his feet. It is the symbol of his status. His arms and legs are bare, his hair is thick and curly, and he carries a large black leather shield with a buffalo tail at its centre, the emblem of command. Attached to his waist is a large two-edged knife in a leather pouch, and in his hand, he holds a spear with a copper plate, symbol of the army general... The group of natives from Assab, our compatriots, is in Genoa awaiting instructions from both the Executive Committee of the Exhibition and the Ministry of Foreign Affairs. Today, Mr Tarchi, representative of the Royal Commissioner in Assab, who is accompanying the Dankali, and the delegate Gamacchio, who was placed at their disposal, faced quite the challenge in keeping them at home, in accordance with the orders received from Rome. Accustomed to roaming free, our guests wanted to go out and about at the first glimmer of dawn. At lunchtime they demanded that a live ox or a goat be brought to them, because they eat nothing but meat from animals they themselves slaughter. After a long conversation, they settled for some chickens, which they tore to pieces, fighting amongst themselves.[13]

The account by the *Corriere della Sera* correspondent was perfectly in keeping with the image that people in Italy, and more generally in Europe, had of the inhabitants of other continents.[14] He dwelled on details such as the knife and shield that were exotic or that emphasized alienness to the modern world, and the buffalo tail, "emblem of command." Visitors to the exhibition would probably have found these decorations made of animal parts decidedly bizarre, yet at the same time find the bear-skin coat of the Sardinian grenadiers, a corps of the Royal Italian Army, or the cap feathers of the Bersaglieri, perfectly normal. The physical description of the young Ibrahim is much more akin to that of an animal specimen than to a human being. "He is perfectly black," a description that is equally apt for an animal's coat. And his "arms and legs are bare"—a detail that underscores his wild nature for a society that evolved elaborate garments that conceal and had a very complex and castrating idea of what was defined as "modesty." Symbols of prestige are ridiculed, more or less deliberately. The command badge on the spear is described as a "copper plate," a definition that could be applied, the type of metal aside, to practically all the medals and decorations provided for soldiers by the Royal Italian Army itself. Some details are misrepresented, others are magnified, all with the aim of conveying certain messages to his readers. The Dankali "guests" want to visit the city because they are "addicted to the open air," that is, accustomed to a kind of wild state. They are not ascribed the curiosity that anyone would have if they were in a new city on another continent. "Curiosity" is typical of the modern white explorer: for the "explored," only the categories of "caged" or "wild" can be applied.

The last passage about lunch crowns the image on an animalistic note. The requests of Ibrahim and his entourage regarding food were probably related to religious prescriptions. It is probable that they wanted Halal food, as stipulated by the Muslim religion. Realizing that their request could not be fulfilled in late-nineteenth century Genoa, they proposed to slaughter the animals themselves. This request was mistaken for a primeval need to "slaughter the prey." The final scene is described, of course, in the most animalistic terms; a pack of feral carnivores wrangling over chickens.

Just two years after Assab was established as a colony, the Italian government decided to "show off" the achievements of Italic civilization by deporting a few of the local inhabitants from Assab as "specimens" to be exhibited at the Italian General Exhibition.

The exhibition held in Turin that year was the kingdom's first major national exhibition, modelled on the great universal exhibitions held in major capitals from the mid-nineteenth century onwards. The event was to showcase the achievements of Italian modernity and, among these, the country's colonial experience was to stand out clearly. The young prince Ibrahim and his three companions were the centrepiece of the display designed to show Italians the results of the export of civilization. Defined as "compatriots" in a liberal burst of inspiration by the *Corriere della Sera* correspondent, they serve to consolidate the image of the tamed savage in the public imagination, the proud African warrior who, like Robinson Crusoe's Friday, unabashedly exhibits his barbaric pride.

The description of the *Corriere* journalist reveals not only the general public's unpreparedness, but also that of the colonial leadership in managing the arrival of the "overseas artefacts" in the flesh: their eating habits were misunderstood, their customs unknown. They were merely part of the set-up and the choreography of the huts built within the exhibition. Given its late start in developing a colonial policy, unlike other countries in the 1880s, Italy simply did not have the know-how to interface with the reality of occupied countries. Apart from a few amateur or "proto-anthropologists" such as Sapeto himself, who had gathered knowledge in the field, almost all the civil servants entrusted with the management of the colony had no specific knowledge of these places. This lack of knowledge, which was only rectified with great effort decades later, became one of the reasons for Italy's poor administration of its colonies and a primary source of clashes, misunderstandings, and violence.

"Human zoos" were created in the second half of the nineteenth century to illustrate the public narrative of the colonial reality to European audiences.[15] They were pieces of humanity ripped out of their context, and exhibited for people in large cities, to emphasize the huge task involved in bringing peoples from other continents into civilization. At the same time, the aim was to instil in the public the notion of white superiority. The early exhibitions that used human beings as props were immediately successful. They fed the public's morbid passion for the exotic, the desire for novelty, the widespread curiosity for the alien, and, not least, the unconfessed pleasure of feeling better than other human beings exhibited as animals. Exhibitions that boasted a few indigenous specimens in their catalogue were sure to succeed.[16]

Besides being a publicity flyer, Prince Ibrahim and his companions had another very important function: demonstrate that Italy was among the main players in the partition of Africa, and allow Italians to boast that they, like all other Europeans, were exporting civilization. Exposing a submissive prince and his attendants to public ridicule served as an imperial status symbol—it certified that Italy was among the leaders in civilizing the world. The Turin Exhibition, which was open from April to November, was an enormous success, welcoming around three million visitors.[17]

The formula was a winner: human beings exhibited as objects became a staple of other major Italian exhibitions. In 1911, eight black figures[18] were again transferred to Turin to bring to life the "Eritrean village" reconstructed on the banks of the Po River. The aim was to tell Italians that colonialism, too, was one of the signs of progress achieved through the country's unification.

Prince Ibrahim, his companions, and the eight figures at the 1911 exhibition were the first soothing balm to assuage Italy's insurgent inferiority complex vis-à-vis the rest of the so-called West. Many, many more would follow, right up to the present day.

The Beastliness of the Colonized in Two Symbols: "Nose Ring" and "Alarm Clock Around the Neck"

In the beginning, most of the stereotypes that characterized the perception that Italians had of the occupied derived mainly from outside sources. The hyperbolic stories of unexplored territories, jungles, and savannahs inhabited by ferocious cannibals, adventurers who became rich by finding hidden treasures—the Italian collective imagination was nourished by fictional accounts that came from the experiences of other country's colonial empires and their cultural reflections. From Jules Verne to Emilio Salgari himself, almost all that was known about the "overseas" world was a combination of incomplete accounts, news features, and lots and lots of literature—often not very good.[19]

When Italians set foot in the colonies, they were confronted with realities that were often different from what they had imagined. The complexity and long history of the social structures, the resources, and the geography of the location itself eluded the newcomers. This incomprehension created a gap that was difficult to bridge:

> They have no awareness of the state of destitution in which they live. What is even stranger is that those who have been outside Massawa, in some civilized centre, return to this life of theirs without regret, with indifference. I have seen several who, after working as servants of officers or travellers—who dressed in

European clothes, ate as we do, and did little work—went from
one day to the next, and without complaint, to the roving life
of before; sustaining themselves with a handful of corn. Their
master had chased them away because, to show their gratitude,
they were stealing.[20]

So wrote the explorer and politician Vico Mantegazza
about the journey he undertook in 1888 from Eritrea to
Ethiopia. Tales like this, following already ingrained clichés,
only made the image—a wild Africa just waiting to be civilized—more plausible. But they also conveyed the idea that
somehow civilization was a futile endeavour, doomed to failure. The colonized seemed biologically resistant to progress.
All that could really be done in the colony was take possession of raw materials, which would otherwise be wasted, and
civilize the land rather than the people.

The encounter between Europeans, in this case Italians,
and colonized peoples very often resulted in a culture shock.
Because of the large gap, the reality of coming face to face
with the Other only reinforced Europeans' many prejudices
and stereotypes, accumulated before the encounter.

Here, it might be interesting to analyze an expression
that entered everyday Italian slang, nourished over time as
colonial exploration moved forward. "I don't have a nose
ring!" is an expression that was once widespread, and is still
occasionally heard in the spoken language. Basically, it means
that "you can't fool me that easily!" or "I'm not stupid!" It is
a colloquial expression, like many others, that also found its
way, and persisted until recently, in journalistic and literary
contexts. The saying has a very long history, with origins in
the peasant world. Piercing the nostrils of large animals, such
as cattle or trained bears, with metal rings to make them
more compliant is a very ancient custom. The pain caused
by pulling on the ring is such that it induces beasts of burden
or entertainment animals to move passively and follow the
handler's orders. Even the most powerful bull or bear can be

controlled by painful tugs at a ring that tears at their nostrils. Animals that are potentially dangerous, "stupidly" follow their handler's orders without disobeying.

To say, "I don't have a nose ring!" is to say that I will not be easily misled. The expression originated in the rural world, but became widespread over time as people from different social settings, so to speak, intermingled. In fact, there are many people around the world who, for cultural reasons, decorate their noses with objects—rings, plates, and precious stones—so much so that it has become a field of study.

> The nose, with its elasticity and softness, has appealed to the *vandalistic* ambitions of many races. There is much evidence for this. The women of the Toubou people in North Africa pierce the right nostril and insert a piece of coral. Among the Barabras people of Africa, the rich sometimes wear a nose ring. In Zanzibar, young girls wear a small ring in the lower part of the septum, which they call *p'heti-ia-pouca* (nose ring). Women, on the other hand, wear a kind of button on their face above the nose fins. The women and children of Labiar wear gold rings decorated with pearls or glass on their noses. The women of Kattivar wear a ring with precious or fake stones on their noses, which is so heavy that it lowers their noses to their lips. Isaiah and Ezekiel speak of peoples who wore rings in their noses. All the women of Nubia wear copper rings with glass trinkets on their noses. Those who can wear two or three rings are happy. In Tallaboutchia, boys wear nose rings. The islanders of Rossel (Australia) pass a bone or piece of wood through the septum. This custom is almost unknown in New Caledonia. While the nose is tormented more often in Africa, in America people prefer to torture the lips. (*Gazzetta medica italiana*, 1862)[21]

Nose decorations were not widespread, and still aren't, among Europeans, who saw these as an element of otherness, far removed from their reality, and a strong symbol of diversity. The excerpt from the medical article quoted above defined these practices, no less, as "torture" and "torment." The editor of the article, stuck in a Eurocentric perspective, failed to see the parallel with a custom that was quite widespread among Europeans—that of piercing earlobes, particularly for women, again for decorative reasons. In all likelihood, none of the readers of the *Gazzetta medica italiana* of 1862 would have described this as "vandalism."

As we have seen, for the European commoner the practice of putting on nose rings was only for animals (such as cattle, and mainly for the purpose of identification), but even in this case the parallel does not click.

The conceptual leap was very short: animals wear nose rings; animals are big and stupid; hence, humans who wear nose rings are beasts. Nubian women or wealthy Barabras people reveal their primitive essences through decorations attributed to beasts—large and potentially ferocious beasts, but rather stupid ones nonetheless. A simple, often misused, expression gives rise to an entire set of images that casts onto the colonized people the stereotypes of beasts of burden or dancing bears at village fairs.

Almost invariably, in nineteenth- and early twentieth-century (and even present-day) newspapers and advertising, indigenous Africans were typically depicted as having curly hair, wearing a straw skirt and, of course, a nose ring. Caricatures and cartoons aimed to be humorous began to appear in newspapers and magazines that were very effective in disseminating this representation. It was precisely this dissemination of caricatures and comic strips that reinforced existing stereotypes and inspired new ones. As critic Alessandro Scarsella recalls: "simply and generally speaking, in comic strips the relationship with reality is always allusive and indirect, since this reality is mediated by previous models which are perceived as examples. From the caricature, a new stereotype can be born that, in turn, functions as a model for parody."[22]

If the expression "nose ring" was re-introduced and adapted by the colonial experience, there are other equally strong expressions that derived from the direct relationship with the colonized. A typical example in everyday language is the expression, "I don't have an alarm clock around my neck!" This was often heard alongside "the nose ring" expression and indicates, in essence, "I am not an ignoramus, a fool, a primitive!"

The idea for this expression probably stems from occasional observations and misinterpretations about the use of technological goods exchanged with local people. It is possible that someone noticed that finer and rather complex mechanical objects, namely alarm clocks, were perceived as rare by local buyers. Upon reflection, they probably were, so they were used as decorative jewellery and status symbols. All the more, Europeans themselves, as the colonized were able to observe, used to wear watches on their person, in their pocket or on their wrist.

What inspired the European and, in this case, the Italian imagination, to turn these episodes into idiomatic expressions, is that the locals failed to understand the purpose and value of such objects. In Eurocentric terms, an alarm clock around the neck revealed both a ridiculous way of appropriating technology brought by white people and an inability to understand its complexity. It was a symbol of the inability of the colonized to grasp even the simplest benefits of progress, and an implicit recognition that any attempt to civilize them was a wasted effort. Biological racism, that is, the idea that the colonized populations were not intelligent enough to grasp progress, was just around the corner. Actually, it was behind the alarm clock.

The beastliness of the colonized was emphasized at every opportunity. Despite their valour and loyalty, the Askari—the mainly Eritrean soldiers who entered the ranks of the Italian colonial army—were not proof of the de facto equality between colonizer and colonized; more sadly, they were simply proof of the effective training by the Italian military.

"The work that Italy took upon her young shoulders for the purposes of civilization and history was not in vain, now that these barbarians, who not long ago were marauders without any moral restraint, now manifest such fervour and conscious devotion to her. She knew how to be a civilizer because she is an educator."[23] These are the words of a correspondent writing about the arrival, in Naples, of a contingent of colonial troops who had fought in Libya in 1912.

Under Fascism, racist pseudo-science became state dogma. Magazines such as *La difesa della razza*[24] (In Defence of Race) published articles about the clear racial inferiority of Africans compared to the presumed virtues of whites. "Compared to the European race, the Negro appears less inclined to heavy and continuous labour. He is in a sense more easily swayed than the European by the immediate desires of the senses and, on the basis of present experience, he appears to vacillate between indifference and hopeless depression..."[25]

A *Luce* newsreel of February 12, 1936, describes the ancient city of Gondar, recently occupied by Italian troops. In extolling its beauty, the narrator describes the city's romantic sunsets. The accompanying images are of a black couple embracing, followed by a couple of monkeys perched on a wall. The comparison between colonized people and animals is always present, even when talking about emotions.[26]

Shapeless Masses with No History. Somalis, Libyans, Abyssinians: One Face, One Race, Inferior

> On a world map, Africa appears before us as more primitive and stout than any other part of the world, except Australia. As we have already noted, its configuration vividly recalls that of Australia and South America, and it is far behind Europe and Asia—and North America as well—in terms of the gracefulness of its contours.[27]

Figure 3. Italian East Africa

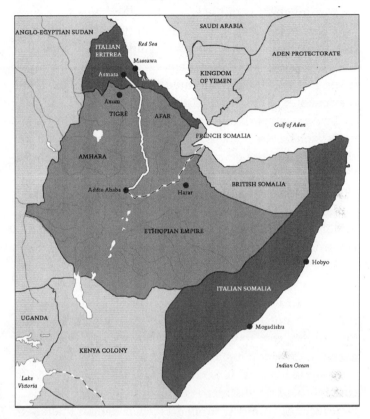

Africa is coarse even in its geographical form. Alongside the contempt for diversity and the denial of the humanity of the colonized—transferred down to the masses by (failed) experiences and widespread stereotypes—there was absolutely no desire to learn about the places and people that Italians otherwise claimed to dominate.

One of the strongest and most ingrained stereotypes among Italians towards non-Europeans, in general, and the peoples that Italy colonized, in particular, was the absolute denial of their unique complexity. It was staunchly, though wrongly, believed that there were no differences between the various inhabitants of the lands that Italy came to occupy. Once again, it is language that reveals just how little attention the Italian colonial approach paid to the dynamics of diversity. The first indicator of this repudiation of complexity is the fact that Italians invented new names for the lands they conquered.

Eritrea is the first and most striking example. The Italian possessions scattered between Assab, Massawa, and Asmara constituted a mosaic of socio-cultural and ethnic realities, and were anything but uniform—from the small sultanates along the coast, to the grazing territories of the hinterland, to the slopes of the Ethiopian plateau, with its porous and ill-defined borders, to the sprawling urban centres at the crossroads of ancient trade routes.

An assortment of sites, clans, towns, villages, or simple oases characterized virtually the entire landscape on either shore of the Red Sea. These local realities were blurred or roughly defined by contingencies. At a given time, and unwittingly, they found themselves under the lowest common denominator: namely, Italian colonial rule. For purely taxonomic reasons, it would seem, Italy felt the need to compel these territories to conform to a known standard of reality that, until then, had escaped the parameters of the European nation-state. As a first step, in its desire to build a unitary entity, Italy unified its possessions under one name. The chosen name was quite arbitrary, one that the Ancient Greeks (a civilization truly alien to populations such as the Dankali or the inhabitants of Massawa) used to identify the Red Sea and, beyond that, the expanse of water that stretched from the southern Sinai to the edge of the known world. The Erythraean Sea, as the Ancient Greeks called it, also included the Persian Gulf and the waters of the Indian Ocean. With obvious antiquarian passion, Italy decided to give its Red Sea possession the name of Eritrea.

Of course, they did not ask the local inhabitants, all of whom, not having any right of appeal, became "Eritreans." The exact borders of this invented country were never established, since the Italian expansionist ambitions of the period suggested that anything that could be wrested from Ethiopia could become Eritrea.

The naming of Somalia followed a similar pattern. The etymology of the word is uncertain, though it seems to derive from an ancient expression in one of the local languages that has to do with the act of milking or "giving milk"—a sign of hospitality. It was a word that in ancient times referred to some pastoralist populations and was later extended by Europeans to include the entire territory of the Horn of Africa, from the mouth of the Red Sea to the borders of Zanzibar. The British were the first to officially call the territories under their control at the mouth of the Red Sea "Somaliland." The Italian explorer Luigi Robecchi Bricchetti used the same model to create the expression "Italian Somalia" in describing the coastal territories of Italy's protectorate, namely Hobyo and Migiurtinia.[28] The toponym was extended to include all the possessions that were amalgamated over time under Italian administration.

Even the name "Libya," as we have seen, is an import, a fictitious construction. At the time of the conquest, the Italian military was well aware of the divisions and differences between the various populations inhabiting the Gulf of Sirte. Tripolitania and Cyrenaica were administrative subdivisions created by the Ottomans, and constituted distinct and sometimes opposing power centres. "Libya" was the ancient name by which various peoples on the Mediterranean, starting with the Ancient Egyptians, identified the stretch of land west of Egypt, and which over the centuries came to identify a large part of the African continent.[29]

Once Italy took control of the coastal regions and occupied, at least nominally, some inland areas, namely the region of Fezzan, it began to use the name Libya to refer to the three regions as a whole. However, the self-identity of the conquered peoples was such that, for a long time, Italians themselves maintained the existing administrative subdivision. However, in reports from the colony and especially in newspaper accounts, one more often heard of Libya and not of Tripolitania, Cyrenaica, or Fezzan. The colony of Libya, as a governed entity, officially came into being with a royal decree only in 1934.[30]

Even Ethiopia, with its millenary heritage, suffered from the linguistic distortion of the occupiers. It is interesting to note that before the invasion in 1935, the Ethiopian Empire in particular and the region of the Ethiopian plateau, in general, were referred to in Italy as "Abyssinia," a word of Arabic origin that in ancient times designated only part of that territory. The word was vague and therefore not used by the imperial administration in Addis Ababa in the nineteenth and twentieth centuries. Its use by Italians is significant because it implied a separation between the reality of the Ethiopian state and its historical roots. "Ethiopian" derives from the Greek and literally means "one with a burnt face,"[31] that is, black. The Ancient Greeks used this word to identify all peoples on the southern coast of the Mediterranean, except Egyptians. In classical literature and in modern times, the term has long been used to identify the continent's black populations. Meanwhile, the use of the word "Abyssinia" in newspapers and in official reports—a term that was hardly imbued with the same history as Ethiopia—had the effect of distancing from its classical legacy the empire that the Italian colonialists had in their sights. Ethiopia, as a geographical name, was found in Greek and Latin texts that young Italians studied at school. Abyssinia, on the other hand, was a collective name that could be used to uphold the fiction that these were "peoples without a history" who need to be civilized. Hardly anyone had heard of the country of Abyssinia, except in matters relating to the colonies. Not so coincidentally, following the invasion, the use of the word Abyssinia in the propaganda underwent a radical change. What started out as the "Abyssinian Enterprise" soon became the "War of Ethiopia."[32] Once they were conquered, the Abyssinians could regain their name of Ethiopians. For the Mussolini regime, defeating the Empire of the Lion of Judah[33] was much more rousing than having "routed the Abyssinians." Needless to say, the semantics of colonialism also tended to flatten out the Ethiopian reality—a reality comprised of dozens of different ethnic groups and languages, different religions, and very varied geographical situations.

The attempt at homogenization culminated with the establishment of the Italian East Africa—I.E.A. *(Africa Orientale Italiana* or *A.O.I.)*,[34] which grouped together all the Italian possessions in the Horn of Africa—namely Eritrea, Ethiopia, and Somalia—into one immense national agglomeration. The head of this patchwork was a governor who was given the title of "viceroy of Ethiopia," and whose seat was in Addis Ababa.[35] A geographical area of almost 2,000,000 square kilometres (Italy is a mere 300,000) was placed under a single command structure, at least in theory. This added non-differentiation of identity would have consequences long after the end of the Italian occupation. For example, after the war, the borders of the Ethiopian empire were mostly established according to those drawn by the Italians. Also, post-war Ethiopia claimed that Eritrea belonged to the Empire of the Negus. They based this on the premise of administrative continuity sketched out by the government in Rome. The thesis gained international traction, so that at the end of World War II, all the Italian colonies on the Red Sea were incorporated into Ethiopia—first in the form of the Eritrean-Ethiopian federation, then as a province. Eritrea would only officially acquire its independence in 1993, following decades of bloody fighting.[36]

Over time, this series of formal steps, namely, imposing on the various colonies collective names that were mostly foreign to local traditions, had a strong impact on Italians and their perception of these places. The majority of people, not otherwise informed, saw these new entities through a very narrow lens—often one they constructed themselves—that was based on the European nation-state and, more particularly, the Italian model.[37]

Hence, to Italians, certain behaviours of the colonized were incomprehensible. For example, why would a new guerrilla leader emerge and create problems in another area, as soon as a previous leader had been subdued. Most people did not understand that the populations united under Italian rule were living in dissimilar territories. The Italians found the attitude of these "ringleaders," who surrender only to rise up again, cowardly and duplicitous.

It was beyond comprehension that the many different geographical entities would have different interests. All local people were openly denounced as being treacherous, and for not keeping their word. This narrative was already being advanced before 1936, on the basis of the confrontations on the Eritrean-Ethiopian border.

Thinking of borders in Africa as similar to those drawn up in Europe in the second half of the nineteenth century—namely as solid as the ethnic realities they enclosed (although this representation is equally fallacious)—caused Italians to fail to understand that there could be Eritreans positioned on either side of the border, sometimes collaborating with the Ethiopian chiefs, sometimes allied with the Italians, sometimes indifferent to both.

In this confusion and lack of understanding of territorial dynamics, the racist stereotypes that already loomed over the colonized were reinforced. In addition to having a nose ring like animals, the locals also lived in social structures more akin to herds than "civilized" assemblies. They did not know the value of their word, and they deviously plotted to harm each other, and above all, to frustrate the civilizers in their attempts to humanize them.

As early as the 1880s, the creation of institutions like the Italian African Society (*Società Italiana d'Africa* or *S.A.I.*)[38] tried to disseminate some actual news about Italy's overseas possessions (albeit with scientific limitations and racism typical of the ethnography of the time). But the vast majority of the population remained anchored to a partial and artificial view of what was happening in the colonies. The news that seeped into the newspapers about the colonies was a collection of bizarre facts or events, usually with the colonized as deceitful characters, particularly if the victims were white. The positive news that reached the general public concerned the good that the Italians were doing. This only served to widen the gap between a world of black primitives and villains who fought to remain backward and civilized whites who were good people trying in every way to revive the fortunes of those faraway lands.

Unlike other colonizing countries, Italy's traumatic relinquishment of its colonies, following its defeat in World War II, precluded Italian society from the slightest bit of awareness regarding the process of decolonization. In Great Britain and France, liberation movements in the colonies fuelled the political debate and drove immigration, and it brought an ever-increasing segment of the population into contact with the living legacy of the colonial past.[39] This did not happen in Italy. The Paris Peace Treaty expelled Italy from international imperialist politics, and the subject in Italian public discourse fell into oblivion. Even if Italy continued to maintain outposts in the international arena (such as the mandate in Somalia until 1960), for the Italian public as a whole the colonial discourse was closed. The will to gain any further knowledge about the peoples that were so marked by our presence was abandoned along with the colonies.

During its eighty years of overseas domination, Italy never bothered to inform Italian society about the societies and cultures it invaded and subjugated—not even in the broadest terms. During its years of whirlwind development, post-war Italy had even less interest in getting to know the peoples it once controlled.

As a result of the political upheavals of decolonization, which made borders unstable, Italian geography textbooks presented Africa as a monolith that can at best be subdivided into climate zones—"North Africa" and "Sub-Saharan Africa"—the latter often used interchangeably with the ethnically charged term "black Africa." In Italy, anti-colonial movements and independence generated an attitude of irony, depicted, among others, in the satirical (and very successful) film *Finché c'è guerra c'è speranza* (While There's War There's Hope—1974) by, and with, Alberto Sordi. In the film, an Italian arms dealer travels around Africa selling instruments of death to various local dictators.

The image of decolonization that prevails in Italy is one of Africans intent on making endless war on each other. The Italian collective imagination draws a bleak picture of Africans, though it never tries to explore why certain political phenomena resulted in violence. All they can see is Africans unable to build stable state structures and in a state of perpetual civil war. The barely veiled subtext is that the continent's inhabitants lack the capacity to establish democratic or even minimally efficient regimes. The image of the colonial past is reinforced, and the facts prove it: the colonized "needed" the white man.

Most post-colonial Europeans continued to believe this. In other post-imperial realities, the debate on the colonizers' responsibilities was imposed by ties with the former colonies. But in Italy, the racist charge of post-colonial stereotypes was not mitigated by direct contact with the realities: these were—and remain—mostly anonymous victims of the prejudice. Even today, apart from the occasional contrarian dispatch, the media tends to report generic news and to speak about problems and migrants from "Africa" in broad terms. A continent of 30 million square kilometres and 1.2 billion people living in 54 independent states is summed up in one word.

"Beautiful Land of Love": The Erotic Imagery of the Colony

As historian Giulietta Stefani's seminal essay reminds us, the colony was a thing "for men only."[40] Men were the explorers of the new lands; men were the politicians who decided to occupy; men were the military who invaded; and men were those who opposed them in the invaded lands. Once the territory was conquered, the vast majority of Italians who took up residence in the colonies were men: soldiers, officials, entrepreneurs. The very few women present were the wives of officials and civil servants, prostitutes who followed the troops and the wives, mothers, and daughters of peasants who were given plots of land when the odd experiment in agricultural colonization was successful.[41]

Even at the height of the colonial settlement in 1939, there were a mere 26,628 Italian women in Italian East Africa, more than half (14,827) of whom were in the oldest colony, Eritrea.[42] This compares to approximately 160,000 Italian male civilians to whom, in the period between the invasion of 1936 and the liberation of 1941, we must add more than 20,000 regular army soldiers.[43] In the Libyan colony, at the height of Italy's presence in 1939, the ratio was slightly more balanced: there were 34,200 Italian women—29 percent of the total number of Italian civilians. Again, Italian soldiers must be added to the male count.[44]

This huge disparity highlights the fact that the relationship between Italians and local people in the colonies was inevitably also a gender issue, and this affected the relationships between the colonized and the colonizers.

One of the recurring literary themes, soon to become commonplace, was the alleged sensuality of colonized women. From the earliest accounts in the nineteenth-century, one cannot help but notice the emphasis on sex in the description of the supposed "typical traits" of Africans. In his treatise, anthropologist Filippo Manetta praises the acumen of his colleague Pruner Bey who writes:

> The capacity of the Negro is limited to imitation. The prevailing impulse is for sensuality and rest. As soon as the physical needs are satisfied, all physical exertion in him ceases, and the body surrenders to the enjoyment of venereal pleasures and to idleness. For him family ties are very weak. Whether he is a husband or father, he is always negligent. Jealousy has only carnal motives, and a woman's fidelity is secured by mechanical means. The most powerful motivators in the Negro's life are drunkenness, gambling, lascivious pleasures, and bodily adornments.[45]

In 1895, the illustrated magazine *Geografia per tutti* (Geography for Everyone), conceived for mass consumption and as a compendium for Italian senior high schools, described the newly acquired peoples by the Indian Ocean:

> The character of the Somalis in general is cruel, sullen, rapacious. They consider their women as beasts of burden. The men devote themselves to hunting; those in one tribe will try to steal the others' herds. They guard their territory. They are ignorant, and have no writing system. They practice polygamy.[46]

Even in 1930, *La Stampa* carried an article with the eloquent title of "Le belle donne di Assab" (The Beautiful Women of Assab), which described "beautiful women, naked from the waist up, ... who run away screaming when we appear."[47] In short, sex is always a fundamental characteristic by which to identify the colonized; and in a colony dominated by men, this focus can only be on local women.

In the collective imagination, colonies were places where sexuality was far more dominant than at home, both because of the detachment from European social conventions and because of the "natural" predisposition of local women to sensuality.

There was the myth of the so-called "Black Venus"—a statuesque and sinuous beauty, erotic and animalistic, who became the embodiment of an entire continent. The memoirist Giuseppe Piccinini in his populist, multi-volume *Guerra d'Africa* (The African War),[48] begins by outlining the whole of Africa with this erotic metaphor:

> The Black Venus of terrible and, all too often, lethal embraces; the Black Venus of fatal enchantments, of portentous endowments enclosed in her ponderous, virginal breasts. The Black Venus, who filled the world with her name and aroused the lusts, the conquering ambitions, of the greatest powers of Europe.[49]

This stereotypical overlapping of the land and the women is made explicit by Piccinini a few pages later in describing Abyssinian women: "Abyssinian women are in general very beautiful, the most beautiful women in Africa, but their customs reveal the height of corruption."[50]

All the propaganda, even the most prudish, seems to give a nod to this aspect of African colonial life. With occasional exceptions regarding Libya—perhaps because of its geographical proximity to Italy—the belief was that the overseas colonies were a sexual paradise for Italian men. The women are "easy" and, above all they can be taken by right of conquest; and because they are more inclined to an animalistic sexuality, they are willing to give themselves, especially to a white man. "The hatred for foreigners is such that the Assabine women greeted poor Giulietti with stones, like a mangy dog: yes, those savages were surely fascinated by that handsome white man!"[51] declared a rather astonished explorer, Giovanni Battista Licata, in his 1885 account of his trip to the Eritrean colony.

The women in the colonies are "easy." This was an assumption believed by all men who set off for the conquered lands. In a sense, the inferiority of black women was more easily presumed and manifest compared to black men. If the colonized men could be ascribed with flashes of dignity or feelings of honour, usually by fighting, their women could not. In the imperialist societies of the first half of the twentieth century, the female body was generally an object; that of the black woman, even more so.[52]

For example, in 1934, Turin's *La Stampa* reported a casting call for a film in Mogadishu, Somalia. The Italian production company was looking for a "black beauty." The news item was accompanied by an image of two smiling Somali girls, one of whom was bare-breasted.[53] For the censorship tenets of the time, it was unimaginable that a major newspaper would carry the photograph of a bare-breasted white woman. People would have cried out pornography. But not so when it came to the body of a black woman, which the censors saw almost in the same way as that of a naked new-born baby—there was no prurience intended, or was there? The bodies of black women are like the "bodies of children," that is, not affected by the need to restrain their sexual charge. Geographical atlases and magazines, as well, could publish photographs of naked black women without incurring the wrath of censors. The diversity—read inferiority—of blacks depleted the sexual charge of those images, which were published for purely scientific purposes. Evidently, this was not the case.

The increased use of film cameras and the growth of propaganda films increased opportunities to allude to the erotic. A film by the *Istituto Luce*, dated April 8, 1936, entitled *Documentario sulla regione della Dancalia*[54] (Documentary on the Region of Dankalia), in Eritrea, showed images of local girls "in search of water." While the narrator describes the importance of water as a resource and of the population's hardship due to drought, the camera focuses on half-naked girls bathing at a spring. One girl, evidently asked by the cameraman to pose, sits bare-breasted and smiling at the camera for a few very long seconds. In virtually all "ethnographic" documentaries of the time, one finds images of local female nudity, presented as part of the "sensual" landscape of the colonies.

The fact that the first images of naked women to appear in Italian newspapers, magazines, newsreels, and documentaries are "black nudes" only confirmed the stereotypes about the sensuality of the colonized. The very fact of posing with bare breasts was, for the Italian morality of the time, empirical proof of the lasciviousness of the women posing. Meanwhile, the image of the fully nude male—even a black male—was a much more enduring taboo in Italian culture.

There is no cultural context—for example, the image of mothers not covering their bodies to breastfeed their children—in which this nudity can be justified. Nudity is seen as having one objective: provocation.

This view becomes the cornerstone of the constant devaluation of the black female body. The unequal exposure of the female body in Italian popular culture continued well after the end of Italian colonialism. In cinema, for decades the myth of the "Black Venus" was enough justification to show black women completely nude—with nary a word from censors. Bare-breasted black women appeared in Italian films for general audiences throughout the 1960s and 1970s, just as debates on the objectification of the (white) female body raged on.

This appeal to sexuality, often used as a propaganda tool, played on the ambiguity of the sexual context to make the colony seem a desirable place. Right from the start, at the end of the nineteenth century, it was the Italian military complex that opened the market for erotic or openly pornographic postcards. As an early colonial superpower, Great Britain was the first and most powerful driving force behind this trade. Its officers, military personnel, and staff had been fuelling the demand for colonial pornography from the mid-nineteenth century. As historian Emanuele Ertola recalls, "the British Empire was described as a vast 'supplier of obscenity' because of the considerable number of pornographic books, photographs, and postcards that circulated from the motherland to the colonies, between the colonies, and from the Empire to the motherland."[55]

Even Italy, though last among the colonizers, succeeded in making this market flourish. Images of naked black women in provocative poses, passed off as scientific or artistic, but more often manifestly erotic, circulated among the military. The material was not subject to censorship; rather it was almost considered part of the good soldier's equipment. Italian soldiers carried pocket cameras for the first time in the Ethiopian campaign of 1935. This unleashed a veritable race to produce "independent" erotic images, leading to a proliferation of photos of smiling soldiers next to young black women, probably stripped naked by the invaders for the occasion. Many who returned home from Africa with these unique souvenirs, distributed them among people in their entourage, which only fuelled the myth of "easy" African women.

But the appeal of the sexual promise to be realized overseas was best expressed in the suggestive songs written to accompany the various military campaigns. The young infantrymen leaving for Tripoli in 1911 sang of the *"Bel suol d'amor"* (Beautiful Land of Love). The words are sweet, hardly appropriate for a military campaign, and they identify the territory to be conquered as an erotic locale. The song's title, "To Tripoli," is supposed to dispel any doubts about the subtext. The song was performed publicly for the first time at the Balbo Theatre in Turin on September 8, 1911, by the famous Gea della Garisenda, who went on stage wrapped in nothing but Italy's tri-colour flag.[56]

The song that accompanied the invasion of Ethiopia in 1935 was even more explicit. "Faccetta nera" (Little Black Face) is a veritable hymn to the sexual conquest of the colony. The song, in the form of a catchy march, was addressed to the Ethiopian woman directly, "slave among slaves," and promised her a special kind of liberation:

> Our law is slavery of love
> But it is freedom of life and thought
> ...
> Little black face, little Abyssinian girl
> We will take you to Rome, free
> By our sun you will be kissed
> You too will wear a black shirt...

The underlying erotic component of the message was such that it became the unofficial hymn of the invasion among the soldiers, and one of the most popular songs of the entire decade.[57] It gradually lost its political connotation[58] to the point that it is still popular today, earning a place in the history of Italian song.

From the regime's point of view, however, "Faccetta nera" had become a hymn to racial promiscuity, so much so that Mussolini himself seemed to want to stop the song's success—but to no avail.[59]

The song's racist and sexual charge motivated the soldiers, who often applied the lyrics to the letter. As the journalist Indro Montanelli (then a young Italian officer engaged in rounding up Ethiopian rebels) recalls, many Italians took a "little Abyssinian girl" as war booty. In a famous interview on RAI television in 1969, he recounted that his little Abyssinian girl was really young—barely twelve years old. A "docile little animal," he called her. The interviewer, Elvira Banotti (1933-2014), pressed him on whether he would ever have done this with a little white girl of the same age. His astonishing reply: ". . . but in Africa that's the way it is. In Africa, they marry at 12 . . .."[60]

This effective disdain for the bodies and lives of black women was also present in literature, and it went beyond any direct experience gained in the colonies.[61] Ennio Flaiano's novel, *Tempo di Uccidere*[62] (A Time to Kill), winner of the Strega Prize in 1947—about an Italian soldier who assaults a local woman in one of the colonies—cannot avoid the stereotypes of woman as voluptuous, carnal, physical.[63] The protagonist is not tormented by the fact that he killed another human being; rather it is the woman's body, with its secrets and potential for contamination, that unleashes his anguish.[64]

The sexual stereotype about the black female body was fixed in the collective imagination, and it transcended the experience gained during the conquest. It was even more entrenched than the classic gender stereotype. In other words, "black women" are different because they have their own norms for physicality, sensuality, and even sexual maturity, which are quite different than those attributed to white women.

Another example of this disparity can be found in the history of Italian cinema. In the debate that emerged in Italy around the subject of sexual freedom, the question was raised as to which was the first widely circulated Italian film to show the image of a naked breast. The two contenders were actresses Clara Calamai (1909-1998), who appeared topless for about a second in the film *La cena delle beffe* (The Jester's Supper—1942), and Vittoria Carpi (1917-2002), whose single breast was glimpsed in the feature film *La corona di ferro* (The Iron Crown—1941). It is interesting to note that, while either of these episodes can be said to have marked the beginning of a new era in self-awareness for the nation's creative artist, it is also true that no one in Italy bothered to mention any of the hundreds of images of naked black women that had been shown in theatres for decades prior, not just in documentaries and newsreels, but in feature films as well.

Again in 1958, the so-called "Rugantino striptease" scandal involved a female body "from the colonies." The dancer Aiché Nanà[65] staged a striptease during a private party, in a well-known Roman club and restaurant, that was raided by the police. The scandal was fuelled by several factors, among them the fact that the party was attended by the scions of Roman nobility, as well as film stars. But there was something more. From the photos that began to circulate in the tabloids, the performer seemed to be a white woman. Newspapers and weeklies that reported the event, invariably pointed out that the dancer was "Turkish." In fact, Aiché Nanà was born in Beirut to an Armenian family during the French mandate in Lebanon. Her dance was performed on a "Mat of Allah"[66] in an atmosphere akin to "One Thousand and One Nights." Although Aiché Nanà was not black, she was nevertheless described as a woman who basically did not belong to the "white" world. On the one hand, the erotic stereotype of her dance made readers understand that those acts were performed by a woman from a non-European world, who was foreign to the morals of the time and, above all, of the place; on the other hand, it redefined the episode within the confines of the exotic, of the abnormal, by contrasting it with "Italian morality." In fact, the latter demanded and obtained a trial against the dancer and the spectators. The episode (rather tame by the standards of our times) was a turning point in Italy's conception of private morality. The striptease by the "Turkish" Aiché Nanà, which later inspired a scene in the film La dolce vita (1960) by Federico Fellini, influenced customs in Italy in the 1960s and beyond. However, it did so not because it raised the issue of women's control over their bodies, but because the "Hollywood-type" scandal—whose main player was an "exotic," non-white character—brought Rome international attention.

When the country finally came to terms with the notion of women having control over their bodies and the emancipatory power of the female nude, it did so poorly—the implication being that the issue only mattered for the "white nude." The non-white nude was not imbued with the same dignity.

Today, decades later, the effects of sexual propaganda are still present in the collective imagination of "colonialist males," for whom the female body is inferior to the male body, and the black female body is inferior to the white female body. This objectification has its roots in nineteenth-century racial theories, but we see its ramifications extend well into the twenty-first century, namely in the Italian distortion of the Black Lives Matter movement.

Chapter 4

Returns

Colonial Memory and Colonial Oblivion

> Nailed to the palm grove
> The moon watches motionless
> Riding the moon
> Is the ancient minaret
> Shrieks, cars, flags
> Explosions, blood! You, camel driver
> Tell me, what is going on?
> It's the Festival of Giarabub![1]
>
> ...
> Colonel, I don't want praise
> I died for my country
> But the end of England
> Begins at Giarabub!
>
> Alberto Simeoni, Ferrante Alvaro de Torres,
> "The Sagra (or Saga) of Giarabub" (song, 1941)

Unlike other colonial powers, Italy was dispossessed during World War II of all its overseas colonies. It was a clean break, and it spared the country the process of so-called decolonization, namely, the arduous passage of territories from the condition of domination to one of independence. For countries with a long colonial history, this transition fostered a debate, however flawed, on roles and responsibilities. Italian society, too, developed a response to the colonial phenomenon. This chapter focuses on the mechanisms through which the country has tried to (not) come to terms with its colonial past.

"Witnesses" from Overseas: Too Many Soldiers, Too Few Colonists, All of Them Revenants

The nature of Italian emigration to the colonies did not favour a meaningful exchange or even a mutual acquaintance between people. The vast majority of Italians who came into contact with the local population were military personnel. Over decades, hundreds of thousands of officers and conscripts viewed the notion of going to a foreign country as a youthful adventure, and this irrevocably shaped the view of the colonies at home.

The multitude of young men who returned home recounted their relationship with the Other through their own biased point of view. This is one of the reasons why, for a large segment of Italian society, Italy's colonies were places with a high incidence of sexual activity, and a combination of barracks, marches in inhospitable places, ambushes, and hostile populations.

The archetype of this narrative can be found in works such as Indro Montanelli's *XX Battaglione Eritreo*.[2] Military service in the colony was perceived and recounted by young men as a gap—a holiday—that preceded adulthood. "For us this war is like a nice, long holiday, given to us by *Gran Babbo* [Big Daddy—Mussolini] as a reward for 13 years of schooling. And, between you and me, it's about time."[3] The quote could be applied not just to the invasion of Ethiopia but, generally, to all the experiences of young Italian soldiers anywhere overseas. All the elements were in place to create a sugar-coated impression of the colonies in the mind of the public[4]—the allure of the exotic, the monetary incentives, and the low-intensity fighting which, in spite of the round-ups and sporadic clashes with local partisans, was nothing compared to the carnage of a world war.

Excluding those who maintained lasting relations with local people (namely, the few soldiers who had children with local women[5]), most Italian boys retained stereotypical views as a result of segregation and the absence of engagement—the occupying troops over subjugated people. All that remained on the way back home was the memory of hostility; of servile deference; of instilled fear; and of perceived duplicity. The overriding thought was not understanding "why we are in the colony," and the general awareness that "we are not welcome." These formed the bases for the soldiers' narratives once they returned home. The "homogenized reality" that spread throughout Italian society nurtured the belief that the colonies were a place somewhere between the epic of Lawrence of Arabia and one of Emilio Salgari's adventure novels.

But there were other Italians, besides military men, who chose to go overseas. Mainly, these were civil servants[6] and—in narrowly defined areas such as the Eritrean hinterland and Libya—so-called "settlers." The economic justification for the colonial enterprise, from the government's viewpoint, was to acquire new lands for settling Italians. Ultimately, over many years the generous incentives by various governments did not yield the expected outcomes.

The best results were obtained in Libya, particularly during the Fascist era, thanks to the colony's proximity to the fatherland and to a massive promotional campaign. Even so, on the eve of World War II, Libya counted a mere 108,000 Italians.[7] After 1936, attempts were made to stimulate civilian immigration, especially for farming, in the newly named Italian East Africa. In 1939, the last year of peace, there were only 165,000 Italian civilians in I.E.A., of whom almost 72,000 were in Eritrea, 19,000 in Somalia, and the remaining 80,000 in the Ethiopian provinces.[8] These settlers, diluted over a population in the former Ethiopian Empire that was estimated at twelve million—to which we must add the citizens of Somalia and Eritrea (one million each[9])—constituted a very small fragment, slightly more than one per cent of the population. Furthermore, the settlers were concentrated in the large urban centres or their immediate vicinity, in what was a vast and diversified territory. They had little time and little desire to integrate with the local reality, especially because being Italian in a colony meant being different, superior. Italians in the occupied African territories, in fact, benefitted from a preferential status over the local population. As was the practice in virtually all European imperialist realities, whites (Italians and Europeans) and non-whites were subject to separate legislation, different penal codes, and different penalties for the same crimes.

Article 4 of the *Ordinance of the Eritrean Colony*,[10] a law adopted in 1903 that would become the model for subsequent Italian colonial legislation, regulated the separate judicial systems between "natives and non-natives,"[11] and underscored the need for such legislation to regulate relations between the two groups. In the regions where the Italian state managed to create a rudimentary educational system, schools were rigidly segregated. On one side, there were the schools for Italian children of civil servants and settlers, who followed the programs of the Italian state. On the other side, there were the schools for the locals, at first managed by religious orders and organizations and, later, by the Fascist regime, which took the opportunity to impart an education that replicated the model of a society divided into classes, and thus serve Italian imperialism. The Eritrea of the 1930s (Italy's first colony, and the one where government directives were first applied) was a case in point. Here, it was self-evident that the colonial school "should have among its educational tasks the creation of identity, a sense of belonging and loyalty; and be more concerned with satisfying patriotic imperatives than educational needs."[12] In essence, the territory that supplied the greatest percentage of troops for the colonial army received an education aimed at training "the future soldiers of Italy."[13]

In Libya, efforts at the assimilation and Italianization of the territory were even more explicit.[14] Through a royal decree of June 1, 1919,[15] for Tripolitania and of October 31 of the same year for Cyrenaica,[16] the opportunity of obtaining Italian citizenship was extended to Libyans who requested it. Citizenship thus granted would allow equality between "metropolitan" Italian citizens and those born in Libyan territory. This was a remarkable opening, but it did little to change the number of Italian citizens in Libya. The population remained rigidly divided between whites and non-whites. Under the Fascist regime, the measure was significantly curtailed, revealing the racism of Fascist colonial legislation. Equal rights between Italians and the indgenous population were abolished. New measures enacted in 1927 introduced the rank of the "Libyan Italian citizen,"[17] a sort of second-class citizenship reserved for local people, which denied equality between "metropolitan" Italians and Libyans, and attributed Italian citizenship only "by right of blood."[18]

Such discriminatory legislation legally sanctioned the distinction between Italians and locals—a form of apartheid *ante litteram*—and created an unbridgeable gap between Italians living in the colony and the indigenous inhabitants.[19] In 1939, the desperate attempt to assimilate Libya by incorporating it as Italy's 17th region[20] only exacerbated racial divisions between Italians and locals: the new law contained a regulation that barred colonial subjects from having Italians as employees.

While the Libyan experiment forced Italian authorities to legislate "separation," the minute Italian presence in the Horn of Africa allowed a de facto apartheid to be maintained. However, this too was underpinned by legislation that distinguished between Italians and colonial subjects, and by the fact that Italians and the local people had little opportunity for contact.

The laws that distinguished and separated Italians from the original inhabitants inevitably led to the construction of a "colonial mentality" among Italians in the colonies. They were the dominant culture, bearers of modern, white civilization come to humanize virgin territory. Few, if any, realized that by establishing themselves as farmers, for example, they were occupying other people's lands. For this reason, it was important to nurture the myth of Italians coming to "build colonies from nothing." The cultural bond with the fatherland was strengthened by the remoteness and—especially during the Fascist era, if not earlier[21]—by being the focus of the propaganda. The settler was, by definition, the spearhead of white civilization and, as such, his sense of superiority and detachment from the natives increased.

For the same reason, once direct colonial rule ended, those who remained in the occupied lands felt both abandoned by the fatherland and besieged by the locals, whom they saw as trying to "usurp" what they had earned through hard work. Many settlers whose operations were not economically viable without government assistance returned from Eritrea and Somalia with a bitter taste, their dreams of overseas wealth in tatters. In some instances, the decades-long Italian rule also resulted in violence against the former rulers. On January 11, 1948, fifty-four Italians and fourteen Somalis were killed in clashes between the local population and settlers during a series of opposing demonstrations.[22]

In Ethiopia, Haile Selassie's government invited Italian civilians to remain and contribute to building a free Ethiopia, but many entrepreneurs and colonists returned home. For most, the African dream of wealth was only possible through direct government assistance. Finally, the vicissitudes of politics dealt the Italian presence in Africa the coup de grace. First came the expulsion of the last 20,000 Italians from Libya under Gaddafi in 1970; then the abandonment of Eritrea and Somalia as a result of internal conflicts. The settlers saw themselves as victims of ungrateful natives, who ignored the efforts of generations of Italians to civilize them. This was clearly a subjective interpretation, driven by defeat and humiliation; nevertheless, it exacerbated the Italians' animosity towards the inhabitants of their former colonies. "Having turned the desert into a garden,"[23] only to be driven away, fuelled this sense of ingratitude.

Without delving into the complexity of a century-old question, the Italian collective imagination became fixated on the Italians as "victims." Images of Italian families disembarking from steamships from Tripoli and Benghazi fuelled indignation at the way the last settlers were treated, and only added to the well-established preconceptions of the colonized as unreliable and treacherous.

The Great Silence

After World War II, Italians came face to face with the brutal changes in the international balance of power. The Cold War left no room for debate on Italy's blunders and responsibilities in its former colonies. The Horn of Africa was incredibly distant; the public saw Italy's Trust Territory in Somalia as nothing more than a reminder of an uninteresting past. In Libya, Italy's former status as colonial master did not grant it any special status in the contest against other international players, such as Great Britain and the United States, in the rush to secure the country's buried riches. Italy's inability to keep pace during the liberation of colonies—just as it had not kept pace in during colonization—relegated any concrete analysis of the past to an afterthought. Prestige had driven Italy's choices when the colonial enterprise began; in the end, it was the sense of failure that hurled the topic of colonialism into oblivion. Even significant events in Italian post-colonialism, however few, were met with a wall of silence and poor understanding of the almost century-long story.

On October 7, 1970, when the newly-installed Gaddafi government expelled the few remaining Italian settlers from the former colony, the estrangement increased. Although the numbers were quite small compared to before the war— approximately 20,000, compared to the 120,000 recorded in the 1939 census[24]—images of the exodus of fellow-nationals, shown on the news, once again reinforced a distorted memory of Italy's colonial experience and responsibilities. As historian Maria Antonietta Nughedu wrote: "A possible objective analysis of colonialism is met by the memory of the abuses suffered as a result of the 'expulsion.' This, in turn, leads to a positive reconsideration of one's *own* past, by virtue of the benefits delivered to Libyan society. In some cases, the conviction spreads that Italians gained nothing from the occupation and, on the contrary, contributed freely to Libyan progress."[25]

Not only was there a failure to come to terms with the colonial past, but the misfortunes of the Italians who had remained in Libya amplified the feeling that Italians had even been "too good" towards the colonized—"ungrateful" as they were to thousands of Italians who remained committed to "civilizing" them. This led to a reversal in perspective whereby, in addition to not understanding the real extent of the damage inflicted on the invaded, the latter were accused of having squandered the opportunity that the Italians gave them. Everything useful and good that could be found in the now independent former colonies was traced to the Italian period. Even today, in articles and reportages from the former colonies, there is no shortage of mentions of how the infrastructures are "still those built by us." Roads are among the most frequently cited. The subtext is quite clearly twofold: the infrastructures made "by the Italians" were well constructed and durable; and, after the end of the occupation, the locals were not able to accomplish anything.

Processing the Loss

In 1946, *La Nuova Luce*—the government-owned newsreel company created under the Fascist regime and formerly known as *Istituto Luce*—circulated a newsreel of men with turbans and North African features working on an empty plain. They are clearing and tilling the land. One of the men, dressed in black and wearing a typical colonial pith helmet, is clearly giving orders. The film cuts quickly to one of the farmers ploughing a field with camels. Another cut shows a pair of oxen doing the same. A male voice, in a tone reminiscent of the news reports from the *Ventennio* (the Fascist Era), narrates over the images:

> The documentary film we are about to present is one of the oldest and most rare: it recounts with mute yet compelling eloquence the harsh beginnings of Italian colonization in Libya; how Italians educated the nomadic and idle Arab in school and in the civility of work. We dedicate this documentary to all those who ascended as masters of colonization after having brutalized and destroyed entire peoples with alcohol and guns.[26]

Barely a year after the end of the war, and about three years after the effective loss of the colonies, a clip from a newsreel reveals the sting with which Italian politicians received the news of the Paris Peace Treaties.

The Italian government was relegated to the status of spectator in the discussions concerning its very own colonial empire, the main protagonists being the victorious powers, namely, the United Kingdom, France, and the United States. The United Kingdom, in particular, played the role of liquidator of Italian decolonization, after having been the sponsor and protector of many of Rome's colonial adventures.

The United Nations intended to deprive Italy of all its colonies, and the Italian government immediately abandoned the idea of returning to Ethiopia. The invasion of the Ethiopian Empire was internationally recognized as one of

Mussolini's greatest crimes, and its legitimacy could not be defended in any way. However, Italy had hoped to maintain control of the colonies previously occupied by liberal Italy. During the Paris Peace Conference, after distancing the new republican and democratic Italy from its Fascist predecessor, Prime Minister De Gasperi himself went so far as to claim that Italy's civilizing experience overseas had merit and should continue. Libya, Eritrea, and Somalia must remain part of the fabric of the nation, under the republican government, so as to not interrupt the enormous efforts made in showing those peoples the path to civilization.

But most of Italy's claims were rejected. The government only managed to keep a mandate over Italian Somalia, though this too was a geopolitical calculation for control of the Horn of Africa, managed mainly by Great Britain.[27]

However, the Italian imprint on the image that the former colonized had of themselves was unmistakable: all former colonies that became independent did so within the borders drawn under Italian colonial rule. Libya constituted itself into a "United Kingdom" under the Senussi Dynasty (which had led the anti-Italian resistance), thereby unifying the territories and peoples of Tripolitania, Cyrenaica, and Fezzan and trying to amalgamate them into a national identity. Ethiopia and Eritrea formed a federation on the model imposed by the Italian viceroyalty. This worked until Addis Ababa's centralizing impulses abolished Asmara's autonomy, and triggered a decades-long civil war. Somalia saw the light of day as an independent state in 1960, when the former Italian territories were united with Somaliland.

In short, all the large territorial constructs created by Italy, however speciously, gave way to what historian George Mosse would have called the nationalization of the masses.[28] In sharing a common past of foreign domination, the former colonized found sufficient motivation to attempt the construction of stable state realities.

Nevertheless, it should be noted that currently (2021), two of the three major colonial entities constructed by Italians, namely Somalia and Libya, are seeing their territory fractured on the basis of ancient subdivisions—Tripolitania against Cyrenaica; and Somaliland versus Somalia—both of which are in a semi-permanent state of civil war. Meanwhile, Eritrea is the victim of a harsh dictatorship. The historical and cultural impact on the colonized was considerable, even after the end of Italian rule.

But what was the impact of the colonial system and what traces can still be found in the collective memory of Italians? The first step is to look at how Italians perceived the end of their overseas rule. According to Article 23 of the Paris Peace Treaties, signed on February 10, 1947, "Italy renounces all rights and titles to its territorial possessions in Africa, namely Libya, Eritrea, and Italian Somalia."[29] Ethiopia, which sat at the victors' table (regardless of what diehard Fascists want to believe), was not considered a colony. This was a hard blow for Italian diplomacy, as it tried to manoeuvre in the post-war morass. The "internationalism" advocated by Carlo Sforza, the foreign minister in the early republican governments, was an attempt, as the diplomat himself pointed out in his memoirs, "by the great powers to create a new world order."[30] But the fact was that Italy did not figure among the great powers, and the loss of its overseas dominions made this clear. Lending credence to a rhetoric first employed by Italian governments of the Historical Left in the late nineteenth century—that colonies were the status symbol of imperial powers—Italy was now leaving this club in infamy.

The subject of colonialism, after briefly being exploited for political purposes, disappeared from the public sphere, appearing sporadically only in the political one. There were more important issues to grapple with at the end of the war. The peace treaty did not resolve the dispute between Italy and Yugoslavia over Trieste and Dalmatia, which would drag on until 1954. At the same time, there were tensions and separatist impulses in other border territories, namely South Tyrol, Valle d'Aosta, and Sicily. The looming Cold War between East and West did not leave much room for an independent foreign policy. Instead of pursuing dreams of reconquering Africa, it seemed wiser to focus on maintaining control of the metropolitan territory.

Once the country acknowledged its diminished international status, colonialism was very quickly dismissed by politicians as a bygone phase. Just as quickly, governments sought to base the new Republic's foreign policy on themes related to decolonization—"internationalist and Third-World-based"[31]—as it were. This was a sensible move, given that the country no longer possessed any colonies. May as well play the card of the European power who is considerate of the new dynamics of what, with an unhappy euphemism, were called "developing countries." De Gasperi himself coined the phrase during a parliamentary debate on the creation of the Trust Territory of Somaliland:

> Accepting to administer Somalia means working for a new world, and being friends with all peoples who aspire to freedom and progress. You have seen how our approach in the last period won us new friendships in the Mediterranean and the world in general. This is a developing world. We do not know where this development may lead, but it is good to stay close to it and make friends there. Now, friends must be the nations that aspire to freedom, that aspire to independence. All this *means resuming the ancient Italian policy, the policy of the Risorgimento.*[32]

These intentions were followed by concrete actions. Looking at the global potential of the United Nations, Italy immediately applied to host the headquarters of the UN agency to combat hunger and stimulate agricultural development—two fundamental themes for progress in the so-called "Third World." (Italy had already hosted the agency's ancestor, the International Institute for Agriculture (I.I.A.), founded in 1905 and dissolved in 1948, an international body created to stimulate agricultural development.) Thus, since 1951, the headquarters of the Food and Agriculture Organization of the United Nations, the F.A.O., is in Rome. By a curious coincidence, the F.A.O.'s offices are situated in the very building that once housed the Ministry of the Colonies.[33]

It's All Mussolini's Fault

Following the redefinition of the country's political priorities, it also became necessary to find a common interpretation of past colonial rule. The answer was quite simple: the massive propaganda effort aimed at exalting the imperial ideal of colonialism, especially after 1930—the high point of which was the invasion of Ethiopia—was carried out by the Fascist regime. Once Fascism was defeated, marked by the failure to dominate Ethiopia, the only possible conclusion was that colonialism was one of the great failures, one of the great shames, foisted on the country's conscience by Mussolini's totalitarianism.

By repudiating the Fascist regime and proclaiming itself anti-Fascist, the new democratic republic born of the Resistance seemed serene in claiming that it did not have to come to terms with its colonial past—it did not even recognize it as its own. This was a conceptual scheme already in place with regard to the memory of Fascism itself. The aim was to offload any and all guilt onto Fascism, and then declare it expunged from the legacy of memory, and thus from the historical responsibility of Italians.[34]

The conservative, right-wing media organizations that survived the end of Fascism and the monarchy—and which in post-World-War-II Italy still carried considerable weight—gladly contributed to the description of "made in Italy" imperialism as divided between "Fascist" and "pre-Fascist."

As historian Andrea Ungari explains, the pro-monarchist press, for example, "always liked to hark back to liberal colonialism with an emphasis on historical figures, events and themes dear to the collective imagination. Even when referencing the period of Fascist colonial expansion, the focus was not on the upper echelons of Mussolini's hierarchy, but on members of the House of Savoy who had operated in Africa—in particular, Luigi Amedeo of Savoy-Aosta, Duke of the Abruzzi, and Amedeo of Savoy, Duke of Aosta."[35]

This scheme was particularly successful, given that in the cauldron of Italian colonialism and government structures, the twenty-year Fascist period is remembered more vividly than the fifty years of liberal rule and the ten-year mandate in Somalia in terms of relations with the subjugated territories and the crimes perpetrated.

It is no coincidence that the lion's share of the criticism of the methods, practices, and consequences of nineteenth- and twentieth-century "made-in-Italy" imperialism were directed at the Fascist regime, and rightly so. The use of poison gas during the invasion of Ethiopia comes to mind. But the late nineteenth-century massacres on the Eritrean border or the mass executions in the Libyan cities "liberated" in 1911-12 were not so easily recalled.

In Italy's public memory, already clogged by difficulties trying to rework the country's totalitarianism, the history of colonialism simply had no place—as if eighty years of forced exchanges and, as we have seen, reciprocal influences, had left no trace in the public consciousness and in the daily life of millions of people. But these traces, though unacknowledged, continue to condition many aspects of the country's life and temperament.

Hot-Blooded Readings: We Were Better than the British

Following the end of World War II, after Italian political and social circles had spent decades running after the model of European imperialism, Italy started to re-evaluate—or rather, devaluate—the distinctive features of British colonialism. In the 1950s, after India proclaimed independence and movements to liberate the colonies were underway everywhere, Italian newspapers filled their pages with reports of the British having trouble managing these transitions. The unrest that followed the dismantling of the French colonial empire, and the recurring violence in Belgian and Portuguese colonies were also widely reported. The feeling was that colonialism in general and decolonization in particular were clearly issues that tore at the heart of Western conscience. However, they did not directly concern Italians.

Italy's traumatic loss of its colonial empire fostered—in the general public as well as in government—a general disinterest in the problems faced by Europeans who were abandoning their colonial garrisons around the world. In the 1950s, the theme of post-colonialism was dropped from Italian discourse. Its direct effects did not seem to concern the country—as newspaper reports that recounted the difficulties and defeats of the now former colonial powers seemed to demonstrate. Thus, on the eve of Italy's "economic boom," the Italian press reported the many British and French setbacks in Africa and Asia with ill-concealed glee.

In 1956, independent Egypt decided to nationalize the Suez Canal, which had remained in the hands of Britain and France since its construction. With Israel's help, the two powers tried to reverse the Egyptian action by force, but they were decisively repulsed by the Egyptians. War was averted thanks to the intervention of the United States, which basically endorsed Egyptian nationalization. The Italian government sided with the Americans.[36] In the Italian press, as in that of the former Italian colonies, the news was presented as a victory of the former dominated over the dominators, of the post-colonial world over the old imperialisms—a "slap in the face" that clearly marked the end of an era. While this reading rhetorically exalted the fight for freedom of the oppressed, it evidently overlooked the fact that Italy had been an actor in that scheme of conquest and still was, considering its mandate in Somalia.

While the defeats of European imperialism were reported in minute detail, total silence on any possible repercussions of Italy's colonial past created the impression that "made-in-Italy" colonialism did not cause as much damage as the others. Not having to deal with decolonization, Italy did not even have to know about the problems of colonization—on the contrary. If documentaries mentioned the former colonies at all, it was to show, almost exclusively, symbols of the occupiers. The architecture of Italian neighbourhoods in Mogadishu, Asmara, or Tripoli became the only lens through which to look at the now former colonies.

While the British wrestled with growing problems regarding divisions of territories they once occupied, and in many countries around the world independence from Britain became a national holiday, the Italian public narrative around what was left behind, especially in Africa, was treated in self-exculpatory fables. Since it was not a violent domestic uprising that drove out the Italians, but the British army, the idea took hold that the Italians were not unwanted by the populations, after all.

This disingenuous reasoning deliberately ignores the decades of determined resistance from the people of Tripolitania, Cyrenaica, and Fezzan, and of the local Somali and Eritrean groups that opposed domination by establishing a balance of power to counter the invaders. Even the 1940-41 campaign to liberate Ethiopia was dismissed as a defeat suffered by the

British. What was fought over and badly forfeited in East Africa was—and must be—a war "between whites."[37]

In general then, in not having to suffer the repercussions of decolonization and not seeing any of the effects of the brutality of the colonial system, Italians concluded that their colonization was not brutal.

The defence of this false image is everywhere, starting with the republican governments, which refused to hand over to international justice Italian war criminals accused of atrocities in the colonies. From the upper echelons of power down to common executioners, the requests to hand over the murderers, made mainly by Ethiopia, remained mostly unanswered.[38] Among these was the already mentioned "Butcher of the Fezzan" Rodolfo Graziani, who was also guilty of war crimes in Ethiopia. He was in fact the instigator of what history recalls as the "Massacre of Addis Ababa" (February 19-21, 1937) in reprisal for a failed attempt on his own life, in which as many as 19,000 people were butchered.[39]

Pietro Badoglio, who was militarily responsible for the 1935-36 invasion of Ethiopia and the use of poison gas against civilian populations, also escaped justice.[40] In the former colonial stage, as much as in Yugoslavia, France, Greece, and the Soviet Union, there was a refusal to acknowledge the war crimes and the brutality of Italian occupation.[41] On the one hand, bringing these figures to trial would have resulted in an international dispute over the responsibilities of Fascist Italy, which republican Italy would have to answer for. On the other hand, there was the risk that the search for culprits would extend far beyond a few prominent symbolic figures, putting in jeopardy the military command structure, and more generally, the government apparatus. The embarrassing continuity from dictatorship to republic would be exposed in an international trial. Better forget it.

The "Official Story"

This deafening silence was further sustained by a segment of what can be described as Italy's official post-colonial historiography. As historian Nicola Labanca recalls, Italy's post-colonial historiography remained meagre for decades:

> As late as the early 1980s, only two documentary anthologies were available, and only three volumes had been written by three different authors attempting to synthesize the history of Italian colonial expansion. Two of these were old views—works by "colonial historians" from the Fascist era, published in 1927[42] and 1938.[43] The other, from 1968,[44] was a worthy but cursory overview "from the outside" by a French scholar.[45]

Therefore, for a variety of reasons, ranging from the political expediency of the moment to an actual disinterest in a subject alien to many, historical studies on colonialism in Italy remained in the shadows. There were also insiders in these shadows whose scientific neutrality many had reason to doubt. Official productions concerning the history of the post-war colonial past were entrusted, by ministerial decree, to experts in "colonial studies" from the pre-war period. In practice, any possible interpretation of Italian colonialism was left to those who helped build its underpinnings. As historian Gian Paolo Calchi Novati recalls:

> In 1952, to guarantee that the history of our colonialism would be spared unwelcome revelations or distortions, a Committee for the Documentation of Italy's Operations in Africa was struck by inter-ministerial decree. The Committee was composed of a number of Africanists of proven colonialist faith such as Ciasca[46] and Giglio, Cerulli, Giuseppe Vedovato, and many former governors or senior officials of the Ministry of Italian Africa.[47]

Over time, this committee produced a considerable number of publications on colonial history and on African military affairs, all of which were dismissed as "lacking any semblance of seriousness and scientific value"[48]—their

objective of conjuring up a positive image of Italian colonialism was all too obvious. The presumed positive effects of
domination were emphasized, above all, for their civilizing
nature. The reports also praised the construction of infrastructure, both those that were completed and those still in
the planning stages, as well as the introduction of elements
of modernity. To avoid lapsing into an apologia for Fascism,
much of the production focused on the period "before
1922"—the colonialism of the liberal era—and then "before
1936." In addition to extolling the achievements, emphasis
was very often placed on the brevity of Italian rule, as if to
absolve it for its lack of effectiveness—thereby implying that
in the short eighty years in which Italian colonialism was in
operation, it did not have time to fully deploy its civilizing
capacity. This interpretation is being regurgitated among the
general population up to the present day.

Over the years, the members of the Committee became
true "keepers of memory."[49] They managed the archives of
various ministries, including those of the former Ministry of
Italian Africa, and made it difficult for independent scholars
to access them.[50]

Thus, for decades the academic interpretation of the
colonial past was based on a solid reconstruction of all the
"good" that was done—or was said to have been done—in the
occupied overseas territories, which obliterated the actual
magnitude of the violence, oppression, and suppression of
identity. As historian Silvana Palma has stated, it is "an effort
of obstinate omission, of removal, when it is not an overt
denial of the darkest pages."[51]

It is no coincidence that this wall of interpretation is
being breached by researchers not directly linked to aca-
demia or state bodies: primarily, and for a time almost sin-
gle-handedly, by Angelo Del Boca's research and revelations.

This entrenchment has also disengaged Italy from the
very arduous evolution of post-colonial studies done in other

European countries, especially Great Britain and France, where scientific research is contributing, albeit not without ongoing disruptions, to a greater awareness of the issues. While in these countries the topic of colonial domination has entered the fabric of public memory, however painful this may be, in Italy the topic is seen as one in which Italians, as a people, only have virtues and no responsibilities—not to mention blame.

"It Was Different in Africa"

This blindness to the colonial past is combined with an understating of the gravity of the atrocities, since these were committed against "natives." Devaluating the lives of others, especially "blacks," is ever-present in accounts of colonial violence. The huge numbers of massacres are trivialized, given that the victims are non-white. Whether it was the 1800 dead in the autumn of 1911 in the first reprisal in Tripolitania, or the massacres in Debre Libanos in Ethiopia, the lives of black people are simply not worth as much as those of whites, neither in their quality—as in the accounts of witnesses like Montanelli—nor in quantity. Eighty years spent dehumanizing colonized populations, combined with the distance and lack of knowledge of places and realities, left deep scars, and fuelled this near-total indifference. Even when the deaths are counted in the tens of thousands, they draw attention to "Fascist brutality" and not to the victims. While it is true that in many cases the violence was perpetrated by Fascist Black Shirts, as well as by the Royal Army and the Royal Carabinieri, there were many instances of violence involving civil servants and ordinary settlers, in what appeared to be an outright hunt for black people. Nevertheless, the very few Italian post-war accounts that do exist invariably identify the perpetrators of these acts of violence as "Fascists" and not as "Italians."

For the "new Italy," self-proclaimed as democratic and anti-Fascist, the memory of that violence and its actual responsibility were completely alien. On the contrary, and rather hypocritically, Ethiopians, Somalis, Eritreans, and Libyans were thrown in, along with the Italian people themselves, in the cauldron of the "victims of Fascism." One of the "bonuses" of Mussolini's twenty-year rule is that all of the colonial system's deformities—even those already present in the nineteenth century—could be blamed on it. Furthermore, comparisons with the bombastic and violent rhetoric of the dictatorship allowed Italian colonialism as a whole to present itself as much more humane once the Black Shirt was removed. Forget all the massacres and atrocities committed in the colonies prior to 1935; the myth of the "good Italian colonialists" was ready to be disseminated.

The Myth of Goodness Requires Proof: The Roads

What immediately stands out in the *Luce* documentaries and newsreels from the 1930s is the amount of footage devoted to public works carried out by the Italians in the Horn of Africa. As of 1935, in particular, there is an explosion of images showing the "new roads" opened by the colonizers.

Fascist propaganda was particularly focused on infrastructure projects in preparation for the invasion. In almost all the regime's newsreels there are shots of roads, bridges, and other road works that were built or were being built by the Italians. Entire photo reportages by the so-called East Africa Department[52] of the *Istituto Luce*, dispatched to the colonies, were devoted to the roads laid out by the regime. Based on this propaganda, one might think that in the 1930s the Italians in Africa did nothing but build roads.

Given the very limited sources of information available on the colonies at that time, the building of roads became an uncontested colonial *leitmotif*—to the point that it survived the loss of the overseas empire. To this day, construction of the road network is among the supposed positive features of Italy's invasions, particularly in Africa.

The myth of Mussolini building roads was a particularly powerful propaganda tool, as it clearly harked back to the ancient Roman tradition: just as the Romans laid out roads to bring civilization across the empire, so too were the Italian Fascists doing it. In actual fact, the effort to build infrastructures was enormous, and—beyond the propaganda— was dictated above all by military necessity. Good roads meant the ability to move troops quickly to the various areas of the colonies to control them more effectively. On the eve of the war, the dictatorship unfurled a series of plans for the construction of an "imperial" road network 5000 kilometres long,[53] to be overseen by Mussolini himself who, from 1937 to 1939, also held the post of Minister of the Colonies. This is a remarkable number, one that must be seen without the halo of propaganda to be interpreted correctly.

In actual fact, of 5000 kilometres announced by the regime, 400 had already been built in Eritrea for military purposes before the 1935 invasion. The ancient Ethiopian imperial road leading from Addis Ababa to Asmara, which was more than 1000 kilometres long, was also included in the count. Renamed "Victory Way" (Via della Vittoria), the road was partially renovated and the rougher parts made more accessible to motor vehicles. However, it could hardly be called a Fascist creation. It was in fact used by the Italians for the invasion, partially upgraded to accommodate automobiles.

The remaining 3000-plus kilometres of so-called state highways in Italian East Africa consisted mainly of caravan trails mended to accommodate motor vehicle traffic. Only a very small part of the road network was actually paved, and gradients and substrates were conceived with military vehicles in mind. The sections in and around population centres were given extra care so as to maintain the image of an efficient roadway system. But numerous casual travellers mentioned the inefficiency and hazards of the network, and the outright embezzlement in the awarding of contracts.[54] In 1938, the high-ranking Fascist Roberto Farinacci indignantly wrote to the Duce that even on the much-vaunted Asmara-Addis Ababa Highway the road conditions were so poor for hundreds of kilometres that they could "give one a varicocele or a hernia."[55] In another note to Mussolini, he put his finger on the cause of the problem, namely that the road construction was mere propaganda, and the fact that the procurement system had become a form of illicit enrichment for the few:

> Whatever comrade Cobolli Gigli[56] may say, the thousands upon thousands of kilometres of paved roads were a tremendous rip-off for the treasury... The permanent roads are being built solely so that they can be presented to the Duce, and the builder can say: "Today, I did this and I did that." Today, after just two years, the roads are mostly in very poor condition. You can't blame it on the rains, because different segments of the Asmara-to-Addis Ababa road have held up and others have not, depending on the companies that built them. There was no one to seriously supervise the technical standards, and billions were lavishly and foolishly spent ... Too many people, too many firms are criminally sucking at the teats of the fatherland.[57]

The degree of inefficiency and waste was also recognized in another roadworks project that the regime boasted about—namely the road across the entire Libyan coastline—from Tunisia to the Egyptian border, and named, as per Roman custom, "the via Balbia," in honour of the Fascist leader Italo Balbo (1896-1940), who had advocated for its construction. The opus was inaugurated in 1937, and was undertaken primarily for reasons of prestige.[58]

What the ultra-Fascist Farinacci brutally highlighted was a system of power typical of the Fascist period: political-industrial lobbies taking advantage of the regime's policies to get rich via public contracts. The result was a much-flaunted imperial road network consisting mostly of expensive infrastructures used as propaganda, and a reality of neglect and waste.

Italian roads in East Africa accounted for more than half of the empire's expenditures, but they produced no tangible benefit for the economy. They became a huge sinkhole that diverted money away from works that could have been more useful for the development of the territories.

The tragic irony is that the few usable stretches of road connecting the hubs of Italy's possessions also became the main conduits of attack at the outbreak of World War II. In 1941, British troops used these very roads to breach the Italian Empire, and accelerate the collapse of Italian East Africa

It seems clear, as dusk was settling over Fascist rule in the 1930s and 1940s, that the main problem lay in the enormous disparity between the declared goals and the actual resources available to realize them. The empire imagined by the colonialists was too vast for the means of the state, and too unprofitable to constitute a real economic opportunity. The aim, then, "was to keep up appearances," and ignore or conceal the problems that could not be handled.

But thanks to the iron grip over information and the distance between Italian public opinion and colonial reality, the façade of conscientious civilization-building remained in the collective imagination—even after the dreams of empire crumbled. Like many other propaganda myths about the *Ventennio* or the twenty years of Fascist rule,[59] road-building remained a memory almost impossible to contradict in the collective consciousness of Italians. This narrative *leitmotif* has helped shape the perception of the entire imperialist experience of the *Bel Paese*.

Memories of the damage were deliberately forgotten or ignored, and written over by recollections reinforced by nearly a century of propaganda that extolled the ephemeral achievements of Italic civilization—but hopelessly distant from the reality of the countries that were devastated and plundered by the occupation. Even when the postcolonial discourse identified Italians as violent white imperialists perpetrating brutalities, the fall-back response was to invoke the arguments conceived by the invaders: "but we built roads for them...," as if these—which at the time were more useful to the occupiers than to the occupied—could compensate for the massacres, the erasure of entire cultures, and the loss of independence for millions of people.

Relations with Former Subjects

Not only were events in the colonies hidden from public view, but we must also reckon with nearly a century's-worth of stereotypes constantly being fed to the public.

The widespread imperialist racism that existed in pre-war Italian society did not diminish with the liberation of the colonies, as it happened in other European countries. There were no substantial flows of immigrants from former Italian territories. This was so, firstly, because, for decades after the war, Italy continued to be a country from which people emigrated, and many emigrants from former Italian colonies went to more attractive destinations, such as Britain, Northern Europe, and North America. Secondly, Italy did not enact any preferential immigration laws for the citizens of its former colonies, as was the case in other countries.[60]

Rather, existing legislation denied citizenship to children of mixed unions. In Eritrea—whose longevity as a colony produced the greatest number of families caught between the Italian and colonized realities—this additional difficulty was coupled with the objective of the new local political order to jettison the Italian presence, which led to the dispersion of a substantial community with composite Italian and Eritrean identity.

In the early 1950s, when the government in Addis Ababa undertook to "Africanize" the Eritrean population and absorb it into the Ethiopian imperial rhetoric, Italy did nothing to support pro-Italian- or Italo-Eritreans. While politicians in Rome debated the status of children born of mixed unions, and what aid to provide, historian Valeria Deplano recalls that, "in late 1952 a communiqué issued (by the Ethiopian government) declared that individuals who had an Eritrean parent or grandparent would be given status as Eritreans... Those with a foreign citizenship would have six months to decide to keep it or relinquish it."[61] In this way, Ethiopia tried, on the one hand, to apprehend the legal issues that a mixed community might generate; and on the other, to force thousands of inhabitants of the former Italian colony to choose between leaving their country to retain the citizenship of the former occupying power (which did not seem particularly willing to support them) or staying and giving up their Italian part of family and heritage.

Rather unexpectedly, one year after the enactment of the Ethiopian mandate, almost all eligible *meticci* retained their Italian citizenship,[62] and faced increasing difficulties of having to live as foreigners in their own land. The government in Rome did not hesitate to flaunt this purported attachment to Italy as proof of the "merits" of Italian colonization, but it did not, in practice, provide any support. The Italo-Eritrean community, already reduced to a few thousand at the end of the war, scattered over the decades and disappeared. Many of those who went to Italy faced immigration laws that made it difficult to have their status as former Italian nationals recognized. Others chose more immigration-friendly destinations, such as Britain and the United States.

In Somalia, during the Italian mandate between 1950 and 1960, contradictory policies were implemented that envisaged the continuation of some form of soft power after independence. For example, the United Nations mandate required that Italy make the administration of the new state independent of white officials, and that it create the state's social structures, such as local schools—something Italy never undertook in fifty years of domination. Two obvious problems arose in the Italian government's handling of the mandate: one was internal and due *to* the ministerial administration; the other was dictated by international politics. The internal problem resulted from the fact that the administration of Somali territory under trusteeship was put mostly in the hands of officials from the old Fascist Ministry of Colonies, without imagining that this might result in a scandal. If the *de-Fascistification* of Italy's civil service was inadequate and insufficient at best, the *de-Fascistification* of the Ministry of Colonies was practically non-existent. Suffice it to say that, when the mandate was established in 1950, the De Gasperi government thought it was a good idea to appoint the last viceroy of Ethiopia, General Guglielmo Nasi, as General Commissioner to the Transition. Under the pretext of his experience in East Africa, an attempt was made to impose on the Somalis the last symbol of Fascist power in the region, who had been in command of extensive counter-guerrilla operations against local partisans between 1935 and 1941, and who was "responsible for the killing of numerous patriots, including women and children."[63] At the end of the war, the Ethiopian government had included his name on the list of Italian war criminals that it submitted to the United Nations War Crimes Commission.[64]

The attempt to name Nasi was an unseemly gesture, to say the least, and it revealed how little Italy understood the process of accountability for its colonial past. Nasi's name was later withdrawn, but the apparatus that oversaw Somalia's transition to independence—the Ministry of Italian Africa created by Mussolini[65]—remained in place until it was abolished in 1953. Nevertheless, its administrative structure would form the basis of the Trust Territory of Somaliland [*Amministrazione Fiduciaria Italiana della Somalia* or *A.F.I.S.*]. The second difficulty in managing this last remnant of 1950s colonialism lay in the fact that the United Nations endorsed the notion that a new independent Somalia be comprised of the former Italian Somalia and of British Somaliland.

This limited the power of the Italian government to influence the emergence and development of the new state in a pro-Italian direction. In addition, other identities arose in the nascent Somali national spirit. The Italian colonial past was not sufficient glue for the creation of a common national memory that would permeate the entire country. Existing and more widespread traits took precedence, above all the Islamic religion, which was practiced by nearly all the inhabitants within the trust. Finally, new "regional powers" came on the scene, namely Nasser in Egypt.

When independent Somalia saw the light of day, on July 1, 1960, a good number of local officials had been trained in Italian schools and universities, but the political situation quickly took a very different turn. The focus became the Anglo-Saxon and Muslim: "The strategy of influence pursued by Italy collapsed immediately after independence, with the Somali government's decision to introduce English and Arabic as second languages in elementary schools, and relegating the study of Italian to a simple prerequisite for access to the nascent University Institute of Somalia."[66] This marginal role was further challenged by the advent of the global contest between East and West in the Horn of Africa. In 1969, a Soviet-backed military coup led to the establishment of the Somali Democratic Republic led by Siad Barre, which brought the country into the communist orbit and swept away the Italian-trained political and administrative class in its entirety.

Chapter 5

Regurgitations
What's Left?

We are the Watussi, we are the Watussi
The tallest of Negroes
The shortest among us, the shortest among us
Stands more than two metres
Here we love each other deeply
We give each other the world's tallest kisses
We are the Watusi
We look at giraffes in the eye
We whisper in elephants' ears
Come down here and see for yourself
Come down, come down here....

Edoardo Vianello, "I Watussi" (song, 1963)

Eighty years of Italian rule over vast overseas territories, distorted by distance and propaganda, left a significant imprint on the structure of Italian society. Politics and economics, no less than culture and mindset were modified by the contact—demanded, unintended or overlooked—between Italy and the realities Italy dominated. This chapter brings into focus the most discernible aspects of this contact.

A Century Is Hard to Erase

What did the Italian imagination retain from the century-long construct created by colonialism after the collapse of Italy's empire?

In international politics, Italy's post-war history was marked by the bitter abandonment of its former colonies, which were taken over by other powers (Great Britain, the United States, the Soviet Union, and Ethiopia)—and which, one by one, became engulfed in movements to free themselves from the yoke of imperialism. Domestically, this history of colonialism was more or less marked by a prolonged period of voluntary amnesia.

The small number and low political profile of people from former colonies did not favour the emergence of identifiable communities in Italy that were aware of their pluralistic identity, except in Rome,[1] under specific circumstances. The souvenir of the colony was drawn from the memory of individuals, namely white males who returned with mythologized and highly subjective experiences, or accounts of expelled communities who, as in the Libyan case, reinforced the idea of a brutal expulsion from a so-called Eden.

However, the underlying ideological infrastructure of colonial culture was not shaken in any way. For a long time, Italians continued to live within the propaganda bubble created at the end of the nineteenth century. The underlying images by which the otherness of the non-European world was recognized were still those of white supremacy, especially with regard to Africa.

Words, Words, Words: *Ambaradan*, *Tucùl*, Menelik's Tongue

Spoken language is one of the expressions of this detachment: it creates negative perceptions of the other and solidifies them from very early on.

Small but clearly embedded signals in the creation of mass culture can spread quickly, especially when contact with the diversity of the colonized becomes complicated. Let's look at the example of the party horn, a toy used to amuse children during *carnevale*, made of coiled wire covered with paper. When you blow into it, the sound that is emitted resembles flatulence and the wire and paper unfurl like a tongue. The French call it *langue de belle-mere* (mother-in-law's tongue); the Spaniards call it *matasuegras* (mother-in-law killer). In Italian it is known and marketed as *Menelik's tongue*. The reference goes back to the Treaty of Uccialli (1889), by which the Italians thought they had wrested acceptance of a protectorate over the Ethiopian Empire, only to be immediately contradicted by the diplomacy of Emperor Menelik II. The Italian media went on to portray Menelik II as a liar and cheat—traits generally attributed to Africans. And the toy that elsewhere in Europe takes its name from stereotypes about mothers-in-law and stepmothers, in Italy, is still associated with the figure of the Ethiopian emperor.

There are many examples of expressions still used today that stem from Italy's special—or failed—relationship with its overseas colonies. For example, we still use the expression *ambaradan* to indicate chaos or mayhem. The *Zingarelli Dictionary of the Italian Language* reports its origin as deriving from "Amba Aradam, a table mountain in Ethiopia near where Italian troops defeated the Abyssinian army in 1936, in a bloody battle."[2] *De Mauro's Dictionary of the Italian Language* describes the term as a humorous synonym for "commotion."[3] What was reported as a "bloody battle" that gave rise to a "humorous" expression was actually a massacre (from February 10 to 19, 1936) during which the Italian army, led by Pietro Badoglio, used poison gas and other chemical agents, in violation of the conventions of war, to defeat the Ethiopian army. The Italians suffered 800 dead, while Ethiopian losses amounted to more than 6000 dead and 12,000 wounded. The Italian Air Force continued to drop bombs for days after the battle—as much as sixty tons of mustard gas[4]—on the retreating columns of Ethiopians, which included not just the soldiers of the Negus's army, but also fleeing civilians. By the time the aggression ceased, an estimated 20,000 Ethiopian soldiers and civilians had been killed.

Thus, a reference to an actual war crime entered the Italian language as a quasi-humorous expression that now pervades the culture. Only recently have there been doubts about the appropriateness of the term,[5] thanks to a re-evaluation of Italy's colonial past through TV shows and novels.[6] In 2020 an initiative led by private citizens proposed that the name of the Amba Aradam subway station in Rome be changed to Giorgio Marincola, a partisan born of an Italian father and a Somali mother, who died in 1945 in the battle to liberate Trentino.[7]

The subway station affair is just one instance in which street-name conventions in many locations in Italy continue to refer to a world that is all but extinct, but whose vestiges obstinately endure. The legacy of laudatory names that refer to overseas conquests, proudly— or unwittingly—given to important public spaces, don't seem to jar with the country's collective memory.[8]

Words that Italians use as a result of the colonial experience carry with them stereotypes about the subjugated. The word *tucùl*, which designates a conical-roofed hut used by many East African peoples, especially in the Horn of Africa, has been used in Italian from the 1950s onwards to describe modest, dirty or shabby dwellings. When modernization in the former colonies led to a building boom, Italian newspapers could not help but use old stereotypes—in a quasi-anthropological tone—to explain the urban development of Italy's former subjects. In 1969, an article in the *Corriere della Sera* about Ethiopia's economic rise was titled,

"From *Tucùl* to Skyscraper." The subtitle continued: "Addis Ababa is gripped by cement fever, presenting itself as a kind of museum of modern construction, with buildings inspired by all forms of rationalism and built by Germans, Scandinavians, French and Italians; young people who have studied in Europe are the most fervent defenders of national traditions and culture—Ethiopians consider themselves white."[9] The last reference—which was explained in the article as the disdain of many Ethiopians for, among others, their Sudanese neighbours—reveals the West's paternalism. To help explain complex local identities, the article uses simple, impactful, yet imperfect imagery—the jungle, "architectural colonialism," and, of course, the *tucùl*.

The word also became the subject of a "goliardic" song, which probably originated after the invasion of Ethiopia, but became popular in Italy in the 1950s and 1960s. "Il pianto di Zambo" (Zambo's Cry), also known as "Buccia di Banana" (Banana Peel) or "La canzone del *tucùl*" (The *Tucùl* Song), has a catchy melody. Its lyrics recount the story of Zambo, a "negretto" (a little Negro boy) who becomes homesick, or, rather, becomes homesick for his *tucùl*, when he sees a banana peel. The verses—all in the infinitive because the stereotype posits that Africans cannot conjugate Italian verbs—are a series of vulgar, mostly sexual, double entendres. In Italian, "*tucùl*" is a pun for "your ass hole." Thanks to its classic ballad rhythm and suggestive lyrics, "The *Tucùl* Song" enjoyed wide popularity, and remains popular to this day. Dozens of versions can be found on video-sharing platforms, with millions of views and comments that nostalgically recall the days when songs like this could be sung "without being labelled racist."[10]

The Other, After the Colony: Portraits in Black and White

Cultural references from the former colonies are more powerful than words, and they permeate Italian society.

Cinema, with its expressive power, is the tool that builds much of the Italian collective imagination.

Films recounting the war in Africa begin only a few years after the end of the war. For example, *I due nemici* (The Best of Enemies—1961),[11] starring Alberto Sordi and David Niven, is about a battle between Italian and British soldiers for control of a stronghold in East Africa. The action and dialogue create the idea of a growing mutual respect between the combatants—a noble conflict from another era. The Ethiopians are almost entirely absent— they, on whose land the Italians and British are fighting. A local figure, a warlord named Ras Degedà, finally appears as an enemy of both Europeans. He briefly succeeds in getting the upper hand, but only through deception. At one point, the former white adversaries band together to escape the black fighters' mischief and threats.

This film, like others from that period, was successful at the box office. More importantly, it ushered in a genre that would gain a great following in Italy, which continues to the present day: that of the clash of civilizations. The film imparts two messages: first, the Italian-English war in Africa was elevated as more noble and "clean" compared to the European massacres in World War II; second, right in the middle of decolonization, it emphasized that whites, wherever they came from, had more in common with each other than with blacks.

The "absence" of the local element in war films that feature a rhetoric of honour and service is typical in Italian cinema. Clichés of war being fought by whites on African soil continue to the present day. A film like *El Alamein* (El Alamein: The Line of Fire—2002)[12] recounts the hardships of war in the Libyan desert without feeling the need to explain why the Italians were there in the first place. This extends to the highly successful television miniseries *Nassiriya*[13] (2007), starring Raoul Bova which, while not focused on the colonial epic proper, still recounts Italy's role in a foreign country by using the same, century-old imperialist clichés. The action centres around the Italian military and the soldiers' needs, feelings and emotions. The local population, wearing ragged clothing, is stereotyped as it was in the *Luce* documentaries. The melodramatic setting in which the white protagonists move is easily recognizable by Italian audiences. The occupied people mostly recognize the "goodness" of the Italian occupiers, and only a few fanatics want to stand in the way of "the export of democracy" (years earlier one would have said "civilization"). Even when local characters are given an active role, it is more so as pretext to reinforce centuries-old stereotypes. In Mario Monicelli's 2006 film *Le rose del deserto* (Roses of the Desert)[14] starring Michele Placido, the main characters are Italian army health workers who provide assistance to Libyan people living in on the edge in 1940. The narrative displays the qualities of the Italians: good, generous, more attentive to the need for humanity during war than their allies (Germans) and enemies (British).

The disregard for blackness is so prevalent in mainstream films, that it isn't even noticed—much less is it part of the theme. This is true even in brilliant comedies like *Riusciranno i nostri eroi a ritrovare l'amico misteriosamente scomparso in Africa?* (Will Our Heroes Find the Friend Who Mysteriously Disappeared in Africa?)[15] with top-level actors such as Nino Manfredi and Alberto Sordi, or in popular B-movies such as *Io sto con gli ippopotami* (I'm for the Hippopotamus)[16] with Bud Spencer and Terence Hill. In the Africa of Italian films, black people wear straw skirts, they live in huts, and women, who are always half-naked, do nothing but smile—elements that adhere perfectly to the image created by nineteenth European explorers.

Two Types of Blackness

An evolution of this imagery occurred with the arrival, on the Italian entertainment scene, of Hollywood productions and, more generally, as a result of the influence of American culture. The result was not a total abandonment or even a re-working of black stereotypes, but rather a kind of splitting of the image in the public imagination. That is, the image of the "colonized black person"—savage and obtuse, who elicits compassion and curiosity—carried on. It was still the caricature of the black person with a nose ring and an alarm clock around his neck. But the pervasive penetration of American pop culture gave rise to the figure of the black person rooted in Western society. He was the "civilized" black, fruit of the melting pot of North American cities.[17]

The idea that whites and blacks can coexist in a "mixed" society was already present in the mind of Italians in the 1920s and 1930s with the arrival of jazz—a genre which Fascism defined as "Negroid music."[18] Examples of black and white co-existence were denounced by the Fascist regime as expressions of an incurable primitivism. They were dismissed as peculiar to the United States, where the millions of whites and blacks forced to live together in a multicultural reality were often in conflict—a context far from imaginable for Italians.

The evolution and diffusion of new figures in the Italian cultural landscape did not alter the perception of colonized blacks. Rather, it was the perception of the "black American" that was broadened and refined. This was first achieved through war films that featured black actors. At the same time, many Italians had seen black men for the first time with the arrival of the U.S. military in Italy. Episodes such as that of Abebe Bikila—the Ethiopian athlete who ran barefoot to win the marathon at the 1960 Rome Olympics—seemed to confirm for television audiences the stereotype of the

African who rejected the "modernity of shoes"[19] and ran like a "primitive savannah hunter." But other examples from cinema proposed new comparative models. Films such as *Guess Who's Coming to Dinner*[20] starring Sidney Poitier—a box office smash in Italy as in the rest of the Western world— challenged the collective imagination of Italians, and created a sharp split between anti-racist theory (that began to take hold in Italy after the war) and existing beliefs about race.

"In theory" at least, people began to feel a certain degree of solidarity with minorities, and they adhered to anti-racism as a value of the new West. "In practice," however, people's inner feelings were still weighted by a century of deeply infused biological racism. On the subject of *Guess Who's Coming to Dinner*, the April 24, 1968, issue of *Corriere della Sera* printed a heartfelt letter by a certain Mrs Milena F., where she confessed that:

> I went to see *Guess Who's Coming to Dinner?* and I liked it. I found it interesting because it shows what we can all see is one of the biggest problems afflicting America, in particular, but all men, as well: racism. I am against any form of racism. However, as I walked out of the movie, where I saw a white woman as part of a couple with a Negro man (and a most handsome Negro, at that) she was about to marry, I wondered if I would be pleased to see my daughter, who is of marriageable age, married to a Negro. My body just shuddered in horror at the thought, and my mind was unable to control it. This was a horrible reaction which I disavow. But I can not stop from asking myself: why, beyond any moral conviction, can one's fibres—one's body, in other words—have a law, a choice, an independence, a taste, that is opposed to the spirit?

In short, Mrs Milena understood that culturally speaking racism is wrong. But the idea of her daughter being with a "Negro" caused her body to "shudder in horror."

The response from the *Corriere della Sera* is Illuminating:

Ouch! You touch on one of the most puzzling problems afflicting man. I am not talking about the racial problem, which is difficult to be sure, but about the dualism that exists in every man between body and soul. There is no point in lying to ourselves. We may choose a way of being and living—by our will, our judgment, our sense of morality—but our body may often thwart it, even reject it outright. How can we explain such instinctive forms of dislike for a given person, for example, whom we know to be worthy of all our esteem and respect? How can we explain the body's refusal to accept another person's quality of skin, of body odour—even though we know we are being unjust in our rejection? Natural, instinctive reactions remain mysterious, but reason must overcome them. Your blood rebelled at the thought of seeing your daughter with a Negro, but your mind condemned you for it. This is normal; do not be alarmed. For us, rejecting another person's skin colour—it is only colour—is a matter of not being used to it. If we had had, I don't know, a Negro wet nurse—if we had had Negro friends—the custom of living with them would prevent us from rebelling in the only way we could allow ourselves, we who reject even the idea of racism.[21]

This is a perfect summary of the rift that characterized Italian thought at the time regarding (but not limited to) the "racial problem." The rejection of blackness is "instinctive," that is, dictated by a natural propensity to be repelled by its diversity. Accepting this diversity instead requires a "cultural" effort, which is a symbol of progress. This stance would probably still be regarded as valid by some people today, though it implies a degree of innate racism in whites. The conclusion evokes the need of getting "accustomed" to blacks as a great way to overcome racism. This is meant to reassure Mrs Milena and the many Italian women attracted to "a most handsome Negro," but otherwise horrified at the thought of having one for a son-in-law. At the same time, the reply reveals the substantial difference between Americans and Italians: in Italy there are no black people, so it is impossible to stamp out this "natural racism."

In short, Mrs Milena, the columnist, and all Italians for that matter, can profess to be "theoretical anti-racists," but not be made to prove it in their daily lives.

Italian media reflected this dichotomy: acceptance of a cultural diversity that can include non-white elements; and the perception that this diversity is not an Italian issue. Television was populated with figures who in one way or another narrated the diversity of colour, but always on the basis of rigidly white assumptions.

Calimero is a cartoon character created in 1963 to advertise a brand of detergent on *Carosello*, the prime time television advertisement break. In every episode poor Calimero, a pour little chicken, is abandoned by his mother because he is black. Despondent over his misfortune, he always exclaims, "This is an injustice!" But he is always rescued by the "Dutch girl." The girl represents the brand of detergent being advertised, and she consoles him by saying, "you are not black, you are just dirty!" She proceeds to wash him, which makes him white and happy again. The "plot" of these commercials rests on the false equivalence of "black = dirty, white = clean," that can also be read as "black = bad, white = good."[22]

The character of Calimero was a hit, a staple of *Carosello* programming until the spot was cancelled in 1977. He continues to appear on screens as a cartoon in a number of children's channels, unrelated to advertising, to this day.

Calimero's success was due to many factors but, surely, among them are his capacity for redemption and his resilience in overcoming life's misfortunes. But the message the little chick carries is that being black is an accident of fate, an injustice, that cannot be overcome in any way other than by physically removing the blackness. In short, the moral of Calimero is that being dirty and being black are the same thing, and being black is a real misfortune.

However, there were other concurrent portrayals that break out of such fossilized, late-colonial stereotypes. New characters were introduced on the Italian scene, thanks to American TV sitcoms. Television programs starring black families proliferated in America in the 1970s. They arrived in Italy nearly a decade later, thanks in part to the deregulation of the television market and the flourishing of private broadcasters. Until then, black characters on Italian television were mostly servants, often in comic roles. But starting in the late 1970s and early 1980s, Italians could watch the goings-on in black middle- and upper-middle-class households in American suburbs on their TV screens with shows like *Sanford and Son*[23] and *The Jeffersons*.[24]

Once again, these public narratives presented situations that Italians perceived as very distant and peculiar compared to what they reflexively believed about African colonial reality.

Bill Cosby cracks jokes on *The Cosby Show* in the role of Dr Huxtable—a wealthy, black New York doctor, while Italians simultaneously see television images of the difficult evolution of dozens of former colonies on the African continent.

Italy's former possessions make headlines almost exclusively because of chaos and violence. There were coups in Libya (1969), Somalia (1969), Ethiopia (1974). The civil and social unrest in the former Italian territories were practically the only news stories reported on the country's screens and in newspapers. Images of continuous violence and upheaval reinforced the idea that, on their own, the former colonized were unable to govern themselves. The causes of these difficulties were ignored, and virtually no one bothered to link the problems to nearly a century of imperialist rule. For Italian public opinion, France (with Algeria from 1954-1962) and Portugal (with Angola, Guinea-Bissau, and Mozambique from 1961-1974) were two examples of the costs of trying to maintain colonies overseas. Both European countries faced constitutional crises, partly because of the wars of independence fought in their colonial territories. In France the Fourth Republic, born out of the rubble of World War II, fell and was replaced by the Fifth under Charles De Gaulle. In Portugal, Salazar's fascist dictatorship gave way to democracy. These extreme cases led many Italians to conclude that the loss of the colonies as a result of World War II was, in many ways, a blessing in disguise.

So, on the one hand there were the black people from the postcards of the 1930s, shown with the perennial nose rings and alarm clocks around their necks, used in awareness and humanitarian aid campaigns. On the other, there was the imported narrative from the United States of black men in suits and ties, leading "Western," even affluent, lives. But they were seen as a peculiarity of American cosmopolitan realities, or of other metropolitan realities such as London and Paris. This was neither exported nor exportable, as it was seen as the result of a set of conditions impossible to replicate.

This duality of views was deliberately read as foreign, and it spilled over into the conception of the otherness of colour in everyday life. Until the 2000s, Italian television depicted people of colour as butlers, drivers, or subordinate individuals. Meanwhile, female characters were often put in roles that heightened their sensuality, thus adhering to the century-old vein of the "black Venus." Their lines are delivered by overdubbed voices that have a nasal quality, reminiscent of the first half of the twentieth century, sounding like Hattie McDaniel, famous for playing "Mammy" in *Gone with the Wind*—in other words, a slave girl.

Because there were so few black actors who spoke Italian at the time, they appeared mostly in supporting roles, which only further cemented the stereotypes. This is the case of actor Isaac George, born as George Oshoba Durojaiye in Nigeria. He became a naturalized Italian citizen, and played dozens of characters in comedy films and television series in

the 1980s and 1990s, though hardly ever beyond the stereotype of the naive servant. In the celebrated television series,
I ragazzi della 3a C (The Boys of 3a C),[25] for example, he plays
Aziz, a waiter for the wealthy Milanese Zampetti family,
where he is often featured in gags based on misunderstandings or on racial stereotypes.

In 1986 Isaac George donned traditional African necklaces
and bracelets to film what turned out to be very a successful
television commercial for a well-known pickled-products
company. He delivers his lines, mispronouncing words, with
what is supposed to be an African accent.[26]

But what happens when—despite the engineered oblivion
of Italy's colonies—international contingencies, as happened
most recently, force Italians, willingly or not, to confront
their past?

This Film Must Not Be Shown, Not Tomorrow, Not Ever!

"Who is the old man dressed in white in the picture pinned
on Gaddafi's vest?"[27]—Italian newspapers asked during the
Libyan dictator's official visit to Italy in 2009. Historians
explained that it was Omar al-Mukhtar, the Senussi leader
of the resistance to Italy's occupation of Cyrenaica. After
further investigating the meaning of "Senussi" and why the
focus was on "Cyrenaica" and not "Libya,"[28] Italians won-
dered if the image was intended as an affront. Many Italians
thus discovered that Omar al-Mukhtar is a national hero in
Libya, and that his execution by hanging in 1931 occurred a
full twenty years after the Italian conquest.

Al-Mukhtar had already been at the centre of a diplomatic squabble between Italy and Libya in 1981, following
the release of the film *Lion of the Desert*.[29] The film, which
celebrates Al-Mukhtar's exploits—recounting the guerrilla
leader's life, capture and execution after a sham trial (Omar
al-Mukhtar is played by Anthony Quinn in the film)—was

funded by the Gaddafi government and regarded as propaganda by the Italian government. The film also chronicled the violence perpetrated by Italians in Libya and laid bare the hatred toward the occupiers. It was banned in Italy for "offending the honour of the Italian Armed Forces."[30]

The extant (one might add, deliberate) unfamiliarity with one of the leading figures of the Libyan resistance—who was a bogeyman for tens of thousands of Royal Italian Army soldiers deployed in the colony—was an evident sign of Italians' lack of historical knowledge and understanding. The Italian government's discomfited reaction to the film stood in stark contrast to the public's indifference.

On December 30, 1981, when the film was released in American and European theatres, Italy's ANSA news agency reported dryly that:

> Italian diplomats in Tripoli expressed Italy's disappointment to the local authorities over the release—in domestic and international markets, particularly in the United States—of the Libyan government-funded film, *Lion of the Desert*, for its strongly anti-Italian bias. A statement released by Foreign Undersecretary Raffaele Costa—in response to a question raised by MSI Member of Parliament De Donno—noted that in retelling the story of a Libyan patriot executed by the Italian authorities in 1912 (sic!), the film tarnished the reputation of Italian soldiers. Costa also noted that the film is political propaganda, emphasizing that the honour of the Italian army, in the Libyan enterprise as well as in the world wars, is historically sealed.[31]

The tone and manner of the news release are particularly interesting. On the one hand, there is irritation at an action that brought international attention to an unwelcome past. On the other, the text tries to minimize, even ignore, the historical facts presented in the film. Omar al-Mukhtar's name is not mentioned—he is referred to merely as a "Libyan patriot." In addition, the date of his death is incorrect—it should read 1931 and not 1912. Perhaps, this was a simple slip, a result of the fact that armed resistance in Libya is commonly believed to have ceased with the end of the Italian-Turkish war of 1911-1912. Whatever the reason for the oversight, the newspapers that reported the matter—and reluctantly at that—repeated the anachronism, added to the confusion, and confirmed the very poor knowledge of the subject. In the hazy past of the conquest of the fourth shore, twenty years of occupation seemingly made no difference.

For its part, the film occasionally produced strident but circumscribed debates about censorship. In 1987, a screening in a theatre in Trento was raided by the DIGOS[32] (*Divisione Investigazioni Generali e Operazioni Speciali*), the Italian law-enforcement agency charged with investigating cases of terrorism, organized crime, kidnappings and extortion. After the raid, sporadic screenings of the film were mostly tolerated. While these remained illegal, they were not hindered outright. *Lion of the Desert* was officially screened on Italian pay-television only in 2009.[33]

Restore Hope, Return to Mogadishu: Savages and a New, Horrifying "Beautiful Land of Love"

Libya dominated Italian news throughout the second half of the twentieth century, thanks to both its proximity to Italy and the communication skills of its dictator, Muammar Gaddafi. Meanwhile, almost no information reached Italy from Somalia for decades—especially after the establishment of Siad Barre's socialist regime in 1969—though Somalia was the last of the non-European territories to lower Italy's tri-colour flag.

The country finally made Italian headlines in 1992, thanks to the violent civil war tearing it apart. The demise of the Soviet bloc opened new spaces in international relations; the Somali crisis offered Italian foreign policy an opportunity.

In 1992, following its successful intervention in Kuwait the year before, the United States under George HW Bush—

as "global policeman"—undertook to bring peace to the
tortured territory of Somalia, through a United Nations
mandate. Italy was among the nations that offered to take
part in the international coalition to "restore hope." The
U.N. mission was, in fact, nicknamed *Restore Hope*.[34] Italy's
contingent was the second largest, after the Americans, and
the mission was codenamed "IBIS."[35]

By then, Italy had taken part in a number of U.N. peace-
keeping missions. Experience gained in military crises, such
as in Lebanon since the 1980s,[36] were an excellent calling card
for the Italian Armed Forces. The government was counting
heavily on this type of operation to enhance its military's
international image.[37] Moreover, Italy was the last Western
power to leave that strip of African territory—and the only
one that, in spite of all the adversity, still had ties with what
remained of the Somali state.

Thus, *Restore Hope* became the first major international
test with historical and diplomatic implications. It was
presented to the country as a new chapter in the now century-old story of the good Italians bringing peace and civilization—in this case, democracy—to a former colony. By all
accounts, the former colony had squandered the opportunity
to be a prosperous, independent nation.

Italians at home were amazed to discover, through
television images and newspaper reports, that Italian was
still widely spoken among Somalis,[38] and that it was one
of the country's official languages. Journalists went on to
detail Italian influences that were still present in Somali
society. They reported that the Italian peacekeeping headquarters had been established on "Empire Street," a main
thoroughfare in the Somali capital, so named by the Italian
colonizers themselves. Thus, street names became a tool to
bolster stereotypes. The notion of "we built roads for them"
was reinforced: Somalis still called streets by their Italian
names.

The Italian public was swamped by articles that told of the military's dual effort: a "robust" pacification (the Italian task force was equipped with state-of-the-art weapons that included tanks and helicopters); and a genuine humanitarian intervention. Images showed armoured vehicles controlling the intersections, while military doctors vaccinated children. With the end of the Cold War, it certainly seemed that the role the Historical Left had imagined Italy playing in Somalia at the end of the nineteenth century, expressed in all those parliamentary speeches—of bringing civilization with the paternal but firm hand of the military—was finally being fulfilled.

The depiction of the Somali people in Italian media was twofold. On the one hand, there were those who "understand the effort that was being made" and gratefully took advantage of Italian kindness. This was conveyed through images of women holding hungry infants, confidently turning to men in uniform. On the other hand, there were the "rebels," namely the militias from the different factions, fighting for control of the territory. This segment was represented by images of men howling, wielding improvised weapons, and clinging to speeding SUVs repurposed for armed confrontations—images not much different than those of fighters shown in the *Luce* documentaries during the Fascist period. The only difference was the weaponry. Instead of spears and leather shields, the fighters were wielding Kalashnikovs and rocket launchers. However, the fervour, the unintelligible shouts, and the close-ups of the savage warriors were the same—all too familiar and easily decipherable by European viewers.

Once again, the colonial double stereotype clearly divided those who accepted the presence of whites and those who opposed it. The Western media in general, and the Italian media in particular, harped on this double narrative—a segment of a population was unwilling to accept the gospel of civilization—but without ever providing the necessary background to explain this resistance.

In other words, there was no point in dwelling on the complexities of the situation on the ground. There was no information that could clarify the historical travails of the Somali territory, of which Italy had been a part. Better to simply present *Restore Hope* as an attempt to bring order to a situation that the Somalis themselves made unmanageable.

This monolithically divided narrative of good guys (us) and bad guys (them) gave rise to what became the most notorious incident in Italy's international mission in Somalia: the "Battle of Checkpoint Pasta."

On July 2, 1993, two columns of Italian military personnel were sweeping an area of the capital, Mogadishu, searching for weapons near an abandoned pasta factory, once owned by the Italian Barilla company. An Italian checkpoint had been set up nearby, on "Empire Street." As the operation drew to a close, the first column returned to the base. But the second column was stalled behind a crowd. As the Italian commission of inquiry reported, fighters hiding in the crowd began firing at the Italian soldiers. The first Italian column, equipped with armoured vehicles, was quickly summoned to the scene. Attack helicopters were also sent to support the Italians. After the skirmish, 3 Italian soldiers lay dead and 21 wounded. On the Somali side, reports of the number of dead ranged from 67 to 187, and the wounded from 100 to more than 400.[39] Clearly, the numbers reveal the disproportionate use of force and firepower. Ironically, in his memoir, Italian commander Bruno Loi reiterated that Italian soldiers were under orders to limit the use of force and avoid harming civilians.[40]

The three soldiers killed received extensive coverage in the newspapers. The articles often emphasized the treacherous nature of the opposing fighters, who used human shields to attack "our boys." This narrative continued to feed the old stereotypes of the "treacherous and dishonourable" black fighters. The narrative of the restrained use of force was also a way to promote the positive stereotype of Italian soldiers as "the good guys," willing to hold their fire for the benefit of the population.

Restore Hope, the first, large-scale international peace-keeping mission since the end of the Cold War, was a substantial failure. After a series of bloody attacks, the entire U.N. contingent decided to withdraw—the Americans and Italians were the last to leave. The mission's balance sheet was disastrous. Approximately 100 U.N. peacekeepers were killed, compared to about 10,000 Somalis. Costs soared: just under one billion US dollars was disbursed in 1993 alone, making the United Nations Operation in Somalia (UNOSOM) the most expensive operation ever undertaken by the U.N.[41]

The Ministry of Defence reported that the Italians killed were, "11 military personnel, one Red Cross volunteer nurse, and two Italian journalists."[42] The two journalists were Ilaria Alpi and Miran Hrovatin, who were investigating toxic waste trafficking between Italy and Somalia, and links between the Italian underworld and Somali criminal gangs.[43] Unfortunately, despite decades of disconnection, it seems that, in certain areas, at least, the ties between Italy and its former colony were thriving.

But there is another, terrible form of continuity between the IBIS mission and Italy's colonial past. Years after the end of the Italian mission in Somalia, reports emerged in the Italian press alleging that Italian soldiers had committed violence against members of local groups. In April 1997, a former paratrooper from the Folgore Army Brigade confessed, for the first time, to taking part in violence against prisoners:

> I was in the Joar and Balad camps with the 158th Parachute Regiment stationed in Livorno. I saw men tortured with electric shocks applied to their testicles, left in the sun without

water, or thrown against American barbed wire that is all made of small blades. Other paratroopers had their pictures taken with their boot against the head of the tortured. We also spent time crushing large turtles by running them over with our vehicles. We did all this without any officer ever intervening. Fascist coats of arms and pennants were clearly visible in some camps. At the flag-raising ceremony, many soldiers, including senior officers, gave the Roman salute.[44]

The Italian public was now aware of the brutalities committed by one of its elite army units during the peacekeeping mission. Some information contradicting the supposed unimpeachable behaviour of the army personnel had already been leaked in 1993. At the time, the weekly newspapers *Epoca* and *Sette* published photographs of Italian soldiers using excessive force, such as beating people with sticks, who waited in line to receive food parcels, and manhandling hooded prisoners whose hands and feet were tied.[45] The matter had been dismissed as the necessary use of force to maintain public order. When he was questioned about the matter at the time, General Bruno Loi justified the actions with the line, "those Somalis were not choirboys,"[46] meaning that the use of violence was justified by the belligerence of the captured.

In 1997, there were new revelations about the systematic abuse of prisoners, regardless of the charges against them. Just being in the wrong place at the wrong time might result in torture. The weekly magazine *Panorama* presented an entire series of incidents that included, not just torture during interrogations, but instances of sexual violence against local women and young girls. It published a homebound letter from a soldier as proof:

> ... the whores come out at night and my mates joke and play around with them, until I too am playing around. We grab them by the ass because they are really stupid people, and then seven of them gang-raped her. They penetrated her with

some kind of rifle shell. They tied her to the tank with her legs spread open, and she was screaming, because of, I think, the psychological and physical pain, because they put jam on the shell to get it in.[47]

The photographs of the abuse caused a scandal, which discredited the armed forces and the very worthiness of peacekeeping missions.

Notably, the words and deeds of the soldiers implicated in the abuses shockingly mirror the attitudes of superiority and insensitivity toward locals from colonial times. As for the use and abuse of the female body, the derision in the words "they are really stupid people" reveals the inability to understand the enormity of the crimes committed against other human beings.

Belief in the racial inferiority of the local population was so engrained that it failed to shake the witness's conscience. The many episodes that came to light as a result of judicial investigations made it clear that the rules in force at home did not apply in Somalia during that period. The lack of regard for the lives of people one was supposed to protect resulted in episodes bordering on the grotesque. To justify the killing of a Somali child, an Italian soldier claimed to have "mistaken him for a warthog."[48] Inquiries and cross-examinations by the judiciary and the defence department revealed a general devaluation and contempt for the local population, echoing events in Ethiopia in the 1930s, and presaging Libya at the beginning of this century. Half a century after the inglorious end of colonial rule, racial stereotypes, born and bred more than 100 years earlier, were alive and well among the Italians going to their former colonies.

Spoils of War: The Obelisk at Axum

The failure of Italians and the Italian government to come to terms with our colonial past is one of the reasons some international disputes involving Italy and its former colonies remained dramatically open for decades. This also regularly called into question the country's very desire to end these long-lasting disputes.

On October 28, 1937, on the 15th anniversary of the so-called March on Rome, a stele nearly 24 metres high and weighing 152 tons, that was carved around the 6th century A.D. in the Ethiopian holy city of Axum,[49] was raised in the piazza by the headquarters of the Ministry of Italian Africa (formerly the Ministry of the Colonies) in Rome. Carefully transported from the Ethiopian city as wartime loot, the artefact was the crowning achievement of the Fascist imperial dream, celebrating the conquest and the misappropriation of a centuries-old civilization. The propaganda model was based on the one used by the Romans, which two millennia earlier had brought home some Egyptian obelisks to celebrate their power. The visual parallel, between the Egyptian obelisks and the Ethiopian stele, was the centrepiece of Mussolini's propaganda regarding Africa.

At the end of World War II, Italy was obliged to return all the cultural property it had stolen. Paragraph 1, Article 75, of the Peace Treaty reads: "Italy accepts the principles of the Declaration of the United Nations of January 5, 1943, and shall return, in the shortest possible time, property removed from the territory of any of the United Nations." The second paragraph specifies that: "The obligation to make restitution applies to all identifiable property at present in Italy which was removed by force or duress by any of the Axis Powers from the territory of any of the United Nations, irrespective of any subsequent transactions by which the present holder of any such property has secured possession."[50] It is interesting to note that this clause is understood as binding for the thefts committed in Ethiopia from 1935 onwards, thus recognizing an implicit continuity between Ethiopian resistance against Italy until World War II.

Following a series of bilateral agreements, the first one signed in 1956—only nine years after the peace treaty[51]—the Italian government pledged to return, among other works, the stele, or obelisk, of Axum. The Addis Ababa Agreement, on the artefacts stolen from the Ethiopian Empire and on the compensation to be paid, stipulated that everything should be done promptly. Reparations in cash had to be settled within forty-five days from the signing date, while works of art had to be returned "as soon as possible." It was precisely on the "as soon as possible" that the still unbroken spirit of Italian colonialism intended to fight its last battle "of civilization." The voices of opposition to the restitution of the obelisk, a symbol of Mussolini's conquest, came from a variety of quarters and for a variety of reasons. Some pointed to the technical impossibility: the obelisk had been brought to Italy in sections and reassembled with steel and concrete inserts; dismantling it would jeopardize its integrity. Others changed the symbolic meaning, suggesting that Ethiopia had officially donated the stele to Italy as a pledge of newfound friendship. Yet another compromise solution proposed to swap the obelisk for the construction of a church in Ethiopia at Italy's expense.[52] Finally, there were the intransigents, who asserted that the stele symbolized the sacrifice of thousands of Italian soldiers who exported civilization: the artefact must remain in Italy as a glorious symbol of those achievements, regardless of what the treaties said. In the spring of 1956, when rumours spread that the return was imminent, a group of neo-Fascist, M.S.I militants, organized a plot to destroy the monument. The date of the strike—some time between April 25—Liberation Day, and April 28—the anniversary of Mussolini's death—was chosen for its symbolic value. However, the affair was foiled by police.[53]

The fierce opposition and the stated technical difficulties convinced successive Italian governments to embarrassingly postpone any action on the matter. The fall of Haile Selassie

in 1974 and the establishment of a pro-Soviet government—
making the former colony a Cold War adversary—and a
cooling of relations between Italy and Ethiopia further dis-
suaded Italy from fulfilling its obligations. The delay would
last several more decades.

In the 1990s, after the fall of the Mengistu Haile Mariam
regime and the end of the confrontation between East and
West, attempts were made to normalize relations between
Italy and Ethiopia. The issue of restitution and, in particular,
the return of the Axum stele gained new momentum. In 1997,
on a visit to Ethiopia, Italian president Oscar Luigi Scalfaro
formally promised compliance with the commitments made
in 1947 and formalized in 1956. He further clarified that "the
Ethiopian people do not have to thank us for the restitution
because it is an act that is coming 60 years too late. We know
what it means to have occupying troops taking things away
and never returning them."[54]

In spite of this unequivocal commitment, many more
years passed. Only in 2002,[55] under the Berlusconi government, did the Council of Ministers initiate the formal
procedures for the removal and restitution of the stele. Still,
voices, such as that of art critic Vittorio Sgarbi, arose to
oppose the move.[56]

The stele was finally dismantled in the spring of 2004,
and its segments stored in a military base in Rome. The last
segment reached Ethiopia in April 2005. It took another
three years for the obelisk to be raised in the city of Axum.
The official inauguration, now on the list of World Heritage
Sites,[57] took place on September 4, 2008.

The odyssey was weighed down for decades by the crossed
purposes of governments and intellectuals, the spirited
reluctance of a segment of Italian public opinion and, above
all, by the inability to come to terms with the injustice of the
monument's removal in the broader context of Italy's violent
occupation of the Horn of Africa.

Even after its return, the stele was the subject of controversy. There were allegations that the Ethiopian authorities did not have the ability to take care of it.[58] Meanwhile, Italian newspapers ran stories comparing the good actions of the Italians, who "willingly" returned stolen works of art, to thefts carried out during the Napoleonic Wars and the Nazi thefts in World War II, signalling that, unlike the Italians, not everyone seemed intent on conciliatory gestures. In short, there was an absolute lack of acceptance of responsibility, coupled with an ignorance of the historical context, and the clear manipulation of facts to, once again, fuel the popular belief that Italians are "good people.

Conclusion

Western arms dealers
Go through borders flanked by ministers
All of you, go and wage war in Tripoli
The choirs of soldiers go skyward
Against al-Mukhtar and Lawrence of Arabia
With popular songs sung in taverns
You know, that idiot Graziani
Will come to a bad end
I have already written a letter to the Governor of Libya

Franco Battiato, "Letter to the Governor of Libya"
(song, 1989)

Among the many half-forgotten chronicles that plague Italy's public memory, the one about our country's imperialist and colonial past is probably the most conspicuous.

Nearly a century of invasions, occupations, and conquests have not garnered any attention in daily public discourse. Yet, the signs of this past are still very present and easily recognizable in the way Italy and its people interact with the rest of the world.

Language, art, communication, literature, entertainment, even the names of streets and squares, carry forth a narrative about "the other" that is smeared by this long historical interlude that began with the acquisition of a strip of desert on the Red Sea—and remains open, judging by present-day conversations about whether or not to use the word "negro" in public.

Because of its history, Italy could, should, have a more evolved position on issues such as the struggle for independence and human rights. As historian Neelam Srivastava reminds us, "In Italy, wanting an anticolonial nation means wanting an anti-fascist nation... The anti-colonial struggle is an anti-fascist struggle, and vice versa."[1] Indeed, our failures in recognizing our responsibility for Fascism are echoed today in relation to colonialism.

The traumatic loss of the overseas domains probably deluded many into thinking that that piece of history could be dismissed without further analysis. Today, on national television, we still see entertainers in blackface who speak by swapping the letters "p" for "b" and "t" for "d" to imitate an African accent. Elsewhere, these forms of racism were renounced years ago. The fact that they still exist in Italy is largely due to the absence of an "exit strategy" from the context of colonialism. Paradoxically—and thanks to a mechanism of erasure—sixty years after the last tri-colour flag was lowered overseas, a good part of the country's collective consciousness is still in the colonies.

When Italians today claim to "work like Negroes" to bring home an honest wage and are terrified at the thought of "an invasion from Africa," they are more or less consciously replicating the lesson from a few generations ago, when their country entered faraway lands uninvited and tried to impose a largely fictitious model of civilization which even they, as invaders, struggled to maintain at home.

The Fascist racial frenzy presented itself as a convenient "scapegoat." It allowed everyone to publicly put the blame on Mussolini and his associates for centuries-old distortions—all the while ignoring the long-lasting violent and racist practices that preceded and followed the infamous *Ventennio*.

Convinced of their own "white superiority" (thanks to their colonial possessions), and their "goodness" (for dodging the agony of decolonization after the war), Italians today are still coming to terms with their contribution to the act of "civilizing," that is, invading a substantial slice of the globe. This contribution continues to weigh on those who suffered from it. The obvious traces of the imperialist imprint are still clearly visible today, although those who can see it are few. Not many Italians know, for example, that the Rastafarian religion has its roots in a certain Ethiopian nobleman by the name of Ras Tafari Makonnen, who subsequently became Emperor Haile Selassie. Heir to the lineage of Solomon, he fought for as long he could. Finally, he had to flee, but he managed to regain his land from the invaders, namely, "us," the Italians.

The cultural offshoots of Rastafarianism, namely reggae music and dreadlocks, are among the fruits of that clash, where the "bad guys," the invaders, are convinced that by building roads they brought tri-colour civilization.

When we look at the tragic situation in Libya and Somalia today, there are few willing to make the connection to Italy's occupation. The violent imposition of borders and identities, the creation and destruction of entire economic, social, and power structures, and the use of divide-and-conquer tactics to pit different ethnic groups against each other exacerbated centuries-old rivalries in territories that later became states by the will of the Italians—and discovered their nationhood in opposition to the Italians.

We have lost sight of what we might call Italy's "historical footprint" in the world. Too busy extolling the Renaissance or the technological achievements of recent decades, many in Italy do not know, for example, that September 16 is a national holiday in Libya that commemorates the killing of Omar al-Mukhtar. Few people know that *Yekatit* 12 of the Ethiopian calendar, or February 19, is the anniversary of the massacre of Addis Ababa, ordered by Rodolfo Graziani. Every year, the people of Addis Ababa gather at the monument commemorating the victims. In Ethiopia, the anniversary of the 1896 Battle of Adua is a national holiday. Probably even fewer Italians know that July 1 is Somalia's Independence Day. Independence... from Italy.

Post-World War II Italy tried to remake itself *post facto* into the standard bearer of decolonization. Italian universities welcomed generations of students from colonized countries, including those from former Italian territories. Over the years, the country's diplomats customarily gave attention to issues of international justice for war crimes and economic development. But Italy has failed to bring to the forefront the fundamental questions about its own historical responsibilities regarding colonization and its missed opportunities to develop entire areas of the planet. By trying to focus attention on the problems purportedly caused by others, it once again aimed to substantiate the image of Italian goodness and generosity—all the while rebuffing demands for real expressions of commitment and involvement, such as the return of stolen art or the recognition of the many war crimes it perpetrated over decades.

In the eyes of the formerly colonized people, decades of policies dedicated to the Third World have not erased the historical responsibilities of a regime that perpetrated one of the most heinous occupations in the sad history of European invasions. These policies have only served to bolster the image Italy has of itself and its contribution to the twentieth century—a vision of the "other" that was interrupted during the period of domination, but which has come to the fore today with great difficulty because of the great global movements.

The fundamental problem today is probably this: from the start, Italy regarded otherness as inferior, subordinate, *slave-like*—not as an element of diversity worthy of respect. "Diverse" people entered the public imagination as savages and mindless servants. Then, they disappeared from public view for half a century—but were still represented in embarrassing, racist caricatures—only to reappear now as a threat: "illegal immigrants and intruders," but never "human beings."

The failure to come to terms with the imperialist past prevents us from understanding the reality of a globalized present, that causes billions of people to move for any number of reasons, some of them rooted in the history of the conquered and, therefore, the responsibility of the conquerors.

Unfortunately, this puts Italy in good company. A substantial segment of Europe seems demonstrably unprepared to grasp the long-term dynamics that European colonialism helped create. This is one of the gaps that needs to be urgently filled in European memory—if for no other reason than to avoid slipping into a racist reinterpretation of a victimized, pure, blameless, and defenceless *Festung Europa*, the "Fortress Europe" imagined by the Nazis.

Today, it is more important than ever to publicly address the issues around the country's past as dominator and invader. Failing to air this part of our history will make it impossible to construct an approach that is aware of the problems of "otherness"—from immigration to the relationship with other cultures, and from asylum laws to citizenship laws, not to mention the perception of the other in our daily lives.

Today, Italy needs to recover the overseas part of its history. This is urgent, as it may well serve to reconstruct, not only a more complete and self-aware understanding of its past, but it will also help address the new challenges that an increasingly vast world, without artificial borders, continues to pose for us all.

Acknowledgements

When we wander in the shadows of collective amnesia, every glimmer of light can help us orient ourselves. For this reason, I first want to thank the many people I have met over the years who brought me fragments and patches and slivers of memories, and uncertain "hearsay" narratives. My thanks go to everyone who told me about an old relative who had gone "to Africa with Mussolini" and returned with a pack of photos and malaria; to those who still whistle "To Tripoli!" because their grandmother always sang it while she cleaned her house; to the old veteran, tank driver in Libya, who was asked, "What was the war like?" and confidently replied, "Sand!..." Thank you, because these relics of memory have long been the only visible objects of a past that is as long as it is forgotten. Though insufficient by themselves, together they are necessary to begin a fruitful dialogue about what has been and what remains of this history of ours.

Thanks to Cristina who, in this new stage of the journey too, was able to glimpse the destination before I did, and pointed the way in her consistently unique and precious manner. Thanks to my friend Michele Luzzatto, whom I insist on calling an editor, who once again was able to put things in order, and guide and advise me. Thanks to Silvia Meucci, because she wagered on this book and won.

Thanks to Carlo Greppi, Enrico Manera, Valentina Colombi, the "hunter" Jessica Ognibeni, Alice Ravinale, and Benedetta Voltolini for their distinctive way of reading my work and advising me. Thanks to David Bidussa, because every chat with him is a journey, and every piece of advice from him creates an impulse to explore further. Thanks to my friend Antonio Trombetta, tireless creator of time and space for reflection.

Thanks to Deina and all the young women and men who travel with me and continue to help me discover the world and myself.

Chronology

November 15, 1869. Giuseppe Sapeto purchases several acres of land in Assab Bay on the Red Sea on behalf of the Rubattino shipping company from Genoa.

July 5, 1882. The Italian government purchases the rights of the land on Assab Bay from the Rubattino company, initiating the government's occupation of that stretch of coastline on the Red Sea.

June 27, 1884. Inhabitants from Italian possessions on the Red Sea are exhibited at the Italian General Exhibition in Turin, for the first time, as "savage specimens" that Italy is civilizing.

February 5, 1885. Following an agreement with Britain, an Italian military contingent takes possession of the port city of Massawa on the Red Sea.

January 26, 1887. A detachment of Italian soldiers on the border between Ethiopia and Italian possessions is attacked by Ethiopian militias near Dogali. It is the greatest defeat of an Italian army outside the country up to that time. There are 430 dead, who will be remembered as "the Five Hundred" by the propaganda of the time.

February 8, 1889. A treaty is signed recognizing an Italian protectorate over the Sultanate of Hobyo, on the Indian coast of present-day Somalia.

May 2, 1889. A friendship treaty is signed between the Ethiopian Empire and the Kingdom of Italy at Uccialli, on the border between Ethiopia and the Italian possessions. Contrary to the Ethiopian version, the Italian version of the treaty states that Italy will control the empire's foreign policy. The treaty is immediately disavowed by the Ethiopian ruler, Menelik II.

January 1, 1890. Italy's various possessions on the Red Sea are constituted into a unitary colony named *Eritrea*.

March 1, 1896. An Italian expeditionary force is attacked at Adua, on the Ethiopian-Eritrean border. Italian troops lose about 7000 men, plus all artillery and other weapons. This is one of the greatest defeats by a European army in Africa and marks a setback in Italy's attempts to expand into Ethiopia.

April 15, 1896. The Benadir Anonymous Company is founded with the mandate to exploit the Italian protectorate in Somalia.

September 7, 1901. Following Italy's participation in the expedition to quell the so-called Boxer Rebellion in China, Italy establishes the Tientsin Concession—an extraterritorial district in the port city that serves as a commercial outpost within the Chinese Empire.

May 24, 1903. The *Ordinance of the Eritrean Colony* becomes law. It contains the first regulations that differentiate between Europeans and locals in the Italian colony and dictates, among other things, different treatment between whites and non-whites who commit similar crimes. The law would form the basis for subsequent ordinances in other Italian colonies.

January 26, 1905. Administrative structures in Eritrea are extended to Somalia, forming the nucleus of what would be named Italian Somalia in 1908.

September 29, 1911. The Kingdom of Italy declares war on Turkey over the territories of Tripolitania and Cyrenaica on the North African coast.

October 18, 1912. Italy signs a peace treaty with Turkey, resulting in the annexation by Italy of the Libyan territories and the Dodecanese, a group of islands in the Aegean Sea.

November 20, 1912. The Ministry of the Colonies is created.

June 1, 1919. The inhabitants of Tripolitania are offered the chance to apply for Italian citizenship. This offer is extended to the inhabitants of Cyrenaica, on October 31 of the same year.

July 16, 1921. The operation to reconquer or "pacify" the Libyan coastline begins with the appointment of Giuseppe Volpi as governor of Tripolitania. A massive military contingent is deployed, using counter-guerrilla tactics such as reprisals on civilians and deportations. The end of military operations and the complete pacification of Libya would be proclaimed in 1932.

December 8, 1923. The newly appointed governor of Somalia, Fascist Cesare Maria de Vecchi, arrives in Mogadishu and undertakes a vast and violent "pacification" of the local power structures with the aim of centralizing rule in Italian hands. He places the territory under a brutal military occupation that would end only in 1928, with de Vecchi's return home.

June 26, 1927. The law that reorganizes the administration of Tripolitania and Cyrenaica establishes the so-called Italo-Libyan citizenship, reserved for the colony's non-white population and limiting their basic rights compared to Italian citizens.

September 16, 1931. After a brief trial, Libyan resistance leader Omar al-Mukhtar is sentenced to death and hanged.

October 3, 1935. Italy invades Ethiopia without any formal declaration of war.

May 5, 1936. As Italian troops enter the Ethiopian capital Addis Ababa, in Rome Benito Mussolini proclaims the establishment of the Italian Empire in Africa.

April 8, 1937. The Ministry of Colonies is renamed the Ministry of Italian Africa.

February 19, 1937. Following a failed assassination attempt on Ethiopia's viceroy Rodolfo Graziani in Addis Ababa, a general reprisal is ordered against the local population, which in a few months results in the killing of about 20,000 people.

October 28, 1937. A stele filched from the Ethiopian holy city of Axum by the Italians is erected in Rome as a symbol of Italian triumph over the empire of the Negus.

May 5, 1941. Exactly five years after the Italians occupied the city, Negus Haile Selassie re-enters Addis Ababa, proclaiming the restoration of the Ethiopian Empire. The date would become the country's national holiday.

November 1943. Following Italy's surrender on September 8, German troops occupy the Italian islands of the Dodecanese. This is the last patch of overseas territory that Italy loses in the war. Nominally, the islands would remain in the possession of Mussolini's Italian Social Republic throughout the rest of the war, but under direct German control. On September 10, 1943, the Japanese had occupied the Italian concession in Tientsin, China; Italian East Africa had been liberated by the British in early 1941, while Libya was occupied by the Allies in early 1943.

February 10, 1947. Italy renounces all claims to colonial territories with the signing of the Paris Peace Treaty.

January 11, 1948. Fifty-four Italians and fourteen Somalis are killed in street clashes in Mogadishu, Somalia. The incident is remembered as the Mogadishu Massacre.

April 29, 1953. The Ministry of Italian Africa is officially abolished, replaced by the Trust Territory of Somalia, which would be abolished following Somalia's independence in July 1960.

June 15, 1956. In a bilateral agreement, Italy agrees to return to Ethiopia a number artefacts stolen during the occupation, including the stele, or obelisk, of Axum.

July 1, 1960. Somalia gains independence from Italy.

October 7, 1970. Following the "day of the vendetta," dictator Muammar Gaddafi expels the last remaining Italian settlers in Libya; 20,000 people flee to Italy.

December 30, 1981. The film *Lion of the Desert*, about the exploits of Libyan resistance leader Omar al-Mukhtar, is distributed internationally. The film receives mixed reviews, but it is banned in Italy as "offending the honour of the Italian Armed Forces."

December 13, 1992. The first Italian military units land in Somalia as part of the U.N. peacekeeping mission *Restore Hope*.

June 25, 1993. The so-called "Mancino Law" is passed: it explicitly identifies and punishes racially motivated crimes.

March 20, 1994. Journalists Ilaria Alpi and Miran Hrovatin are killed by Somali militants while investigating illegal trafficking between Italy and Somalia.

April 21, 1997. In an interview published in Italian newspapers, a former soldier engaged in Somalia confesses to witnessing sexual violence and torture against Somali civilians during *Operation Restore Hope*.

November 25, 1997. On a visit to Ethiopia, Italian president Oscar Luigi Scalfaro officially apologizes for the crimes of Italian colonialism.

April 2005. The last piece of the Axum stele arrives in Ethiopia—sixty-eight years after it was stolen and transported to Italy, and forty-nine years after Italy's international commitments.

August 30, 2008. The Treaty of Friendship between Italy and Libya is signed in Benghazi, whereby Rome admits responsibility for the decades of colonial rule and invests five billion US dollars in infrastructure works as compensation.

February 2, 2017. Italy and Libya sign a memorandum of agreement to manage the flow of illegal migrants in the Mediterranean.

Translator's Note

I was introduced to Francesco Filippi's work when I read his *Mussolini Also Did a Lot of Good: The Spread of Historical Amnesia (2022)*, an exposé of the fabrications concocted by Italy's Fascist regime in the 1920s and 1930s to lend itself prestige and quell dissention—fabrications that are still perpetuated today by fascist sympathizers. *But We Built Roads for Them: The Lies, Racism, and Amnesia that Bury Italy's Colonial Past,* another exposé, this time on the false narratives surrounding Italian colonialism, is a thematic sequel to the previous work, and one I am delighted to be associated with. In an increasingly polarized world, where facts are manipulated and weaponized to instil fear and division, Francesco Filippi's work reminds audiences of the menace of demagoguery

This was not an easy book to translate. The author's conversational tone, replete with heavy doses of dramatic irony and rhetorical assertions, required meticulous treatment. Equally challenging was the Italian tendency to compose long, serpentine sentences that simply could not be rendered in English without breaking them up. One final stylistic challenge was the need to contextualize, however briefly, some of the historical references—from Ancient Rome to the present—that are common knowledge for Italians, but that may be less familiar to non-Italian readers.

But it was the material contents of the book that posed the greatest challenge—not technically, but emotionally.

The author's revelations about Italy's colonial past—of the violence, massacres and other atrocities committed by Italian colonial authorities, all in the name of empire-building—are disturbing and will unsettle many, especially those of us who are of Italian heritage.

It is interesting to juxtapose the modern view of Italy—as a cradle of civilization and purveyor of progressive thinking—to the one seen through the lens of Filippi's book: Italians were not always "good." The apparent indifference of present-day Italians to their country's appalling colonial legacy adds another layer to this sentiment. It's a shame.

I am grateful to Robin Philpot for the opportunity to work on this project. I am equally grateful to Licia Canton, my life partner and friend, for reviewing early drafts of the manuscript and for her unwavering support.

Domenic Cusmano
January 2024

Notes

Introduction

1. As per philosopher Paul Ricoeur's understanding of this term, especially in relation to "personal memory"; see Paul Ricoeur, *La memoria, la storia, l'oblio*. Raffaello Cortina Editore, Milan 2003, pp. 133-87.
2. See (among others) A. Prosperi, *Un tempo senza storia*. Einaudi, Turin 2021; F. Focardi, *Nel cantiere della memoria: Fascismo, Resistenza, Shoah, Foibe, Viella*. Rome 2020; and M. Flores, *Cattiva memoria: Perché è difficile fare i conti con la storia*. il Mulino, Bologna 2020.
3. With Law No. 587, *Concernente i provvedimenti per Assab*, dated July 5, 1882. In *Gazzetta Ufficiale* No. 160 dd, 10-7-1882, the Depretis government decided to take over the commercial rights held by the Rubattino shipping company, which had opened a headquarters in the bay in 1869.
4. Date chosen in the United Nations Resolution of December 5, 1959 (A/Res/418-XIV).
5. Many of his seminal writings, starting with the first, *La guerra d'Abissinia*, in 1965, but especially the series of essays, *Gli italiani in Africa orientale* (four volumes starting in 1976) and *Gli italiani in Libia* (two volumes in 1986).
6. The very same Del Boca reconstructs the contours of the affair in his introduction to Montanelli's book, *XX Battaglione eritreo*. (Rizzoli, Milan 2010).
7. A. Del Boca, *Italiani, brava gente? Un mito duro a morire*. Neri Pozza, Vicenza 2005.

1. Departures: Unplanned Birth of an Imperial Power

1. See G.P. Calchi Novati, *L'Africa d'Italia. Una storia coloniale e post-coloniale*. Carocci, Rome 2019, pp. 72-73.
2. V. Deplano, A. Pes (ed.) *Quel che resta dell'impero: La cultura coloniale degli italiani*. Mimesis, Sesto San Giovanni 2014, p. 10.
3. Here and elsewhere the transliteration of the Arabic names is as given in the Italian texts of the time, in this case in the *Gazzetta Ufficiale* No. 160 dd, 10-07-1882.

4. The text of the first contract and subsequent renewals, until the acquisition of the rights by the Italian government, are given in the *Gazzetta Ufficiale* No. 160 dd, 10-07-1882, as annexes to Law No. 857 of July 5, 1882, *Concernente i provvedimenti per Assab*, marking the government's acquisition of the property.

5. For a brief biographical note, see www.treccani.it. A description of Sapeto is also found in Angelo Del Boca's *La nostra Africa: Nel racconto di cinquanta italiani che l'hanno percorsa, esplorata e amata*. Neri Pozza, Vicenza 2003, pp. 47-52.6. Curiously, the Rubattino Shipping Company found itself embroiled in several key episodes in Italian history. For example, the two ships, the *Piemonte* and the *Lombardo*, carrying Garibaldi's One Thousand from Quarto to Marsala in 1860 were owned by Rubattino.

7. For a detailed comparison between "informal imperialism," which is typically more commercial in nature and "formal imperialism," which implies a determined occupation of the territory and the imposition of institutions imported by the colonizers, see among others, A. Kohli's analysis, which focuses on the British and U.S. cases, in *Imperialism and the Developing World. How Britain and the United States Shaped the Global Periphery*. Oxford University Press, Oxford 2020, pp. 10 ff.

8. For an analytical compilation of documents relating to contracts made by Sapeto in Assab before 1882, see T. Scovazzi, *Assab, Massaua, Uccialli, Adua: Gli strumenti giuridici del primo colonialismo italiano*. Giappicchelli Editore, Turin 1996, pp. 1-50.

9. See G. Mammarella, P. Cacace, *La politica estera dell'Italia: Dallo stato unitario ai nostri giorni*. Laterza, Rome-Bari 2010, pp. 27-52.

10. T. Scovazzi, *Assab, Massawa, Uccialli, Adua*. op. cit., pp. 54-56.

11. The "scramble for Africa" summarizes (in English) the characteristics of the assault on the continent by Europeans in the late 19th and early 20th centuries. For an overview see (among others) T. Pakenham, *The Scramble for Africa*. Random House, New York 1991.

12. N. Labanca, *Oltremare*. op. cit., p. 63.

13. www.storia.camera.it/regno/lavori/leg14/sed393.pdf, p. 5.

14. Ibid., p. 6.

15. The title of an 1899 poem by Rudyard Kipling became the manifesto of racist imperialism.

16. E.J. Hobsbawm, *The Age of Empires (1875-1914)*. Weidenfeld & Nicolson, [City] 1987, p. 83. For overview of the effects of imperialism on popular culture in the Western world, see J.M. MacKenzie, *Imperialism and Popular Culture 1880-1960*. Manchester University Press, Manchester 1986.

17. On the "Livraghi Scandal," see I. Rosoni, *La Colonia Eritrea: La prima amministrazione coloniale italiana (1880-1912)*. Edizioni Università di Macerata, Macerata 2006, pp. 150-57 and A. Del Boca, *Gli italiani in Africa orientale, vol. I, dall'Unità alla Marcia su Roma*. Mondadori, Milan 1992, pp. 435-50.

18. www.storia.camera.it/regno/lavori/leg14/sed393.pdf, p. 3.

19. G. Sapeto, *L'Italia e il Canale di Suez: Operetta popolare*. Tipografia e Litografia fratelli Pellas, Genoa 1865.

20. Ibid., p. 3.

21. "Perché l'Italia è andata a Massaua," in *Corriere della Sera*, ed. 20-21, July 1885.

22. Royal Decree of Jan. 1, 1890, No. 6592, creating a civil administration in the colony of Eritrea. In *Gazzetta Ufficiale* No. 4 dd 7-01-1890.

23. The name is taken from what the Ancient Greeks together called the Indian Ocean and the Red Sea, namely "Erythraean Sea."

2. Arrivals: Colonial Failures—A New Lie for Every Conquest

1. In Amharic, one of the most widely spoken languages on the Ethiopian plateau, the title of "Negus Neghesti," literally means "King of Kings."

2. For an overview of the life of Menelik II, see H.G. Marcus, *Life and Times of Menelik II: Ethiopia 1844-1913*. Red Sea Press, Trenton 1994 (first ed. 1975).

3. See G.P. Calchi Novati, *L'Africa d'Italia*. op. cit., pp. 149 ff.

4. For a brief history of colonial subjects serving in the Italian Army, see D. Quirico, *Storia delle truppe coloniali italiane*. Mondadori, Milano 2003.

5. For a brief introduction to this important topic, from an iconographic perspective, see AA.VV., *Ascari d'Eritrea: Volontari eritrei nelle Forze armate italiane. 1889-1941—Catalogo della mostra*. Vallecchi, Florence 2005.

6. Singular "àskaro" or "àskari," from the Arabic 'askarī, "soldier."

7. At the time, the city had only recently become the capital of Ethiopia.

8. "Treaty of Friendship and Trade between the Kingdom of Italy and the Empire of Ethiopia, Uccialli," May 2, 1889, in T. Scovazzi, *Assab, Massawa, Uccialli, Adua*. op. cit., p. 120.

9. T. Scovazzi, *Assab, Massawa, Uccialli, Adua*. op. cit., p. 138-40.

10. Dògali was Italy's first real military catastrophe in the colonies. It was topped by the debacle in Adua in 1896, both in terms of deaths and press coverage. Dògali remains in the collective and literary memory of Italians to this day. For example, an account of the news of the defeat reaching Rome opens Igiaba Scego›s novel, *La linea del colore: Il gran tour di Lafanu Brown*. Bompiani, Milan 2020.

11. I. Rosoni, *La Colonia Eritrea: La prima amministrazione coloniale italiana (1880-1912)*. Edizioni Università di Macerata, Macerata 2006, p. 166.
12. An inferiority complex that was also perceived abroad. In *Imperialism, the Highest Stage of Capitalism* (1916), Vladimir Lenin describes Italian imperialism as a "poor people's colonialism," a description that would haunt the Italian imperialist movement throughout its history. See (among others), L. Ricci in *La lingua dell'Impero. Comunicazione, letteratura e propaganda nell'età del colonialismo italiano*. Carocci, Rome 2005, p. 10.
13. Among the opposition to colonialism as an act of military aggression is the interesting phenomenon of the Italian women's pacifist movement, which was anti-colonial and anti-militaristic. See *M. Scriboni, Abbasso la guerra! Voci di donne da Adua al primo conflitto mondiale (1896-1915)*. BFS Edizioni, Pisa 2008.
14. See R. Rainero, *L'anticolonialismo italiano da Assab ad Adua*. Edizioni di Comunità, Milan 1971, p. 17.
15. L. Franchetti, *Sulla colonizzazione agricola dell'altipiano etiopico: Memoria dell'onorevole Franchetti deputato al Parlamento italiano*. Tipografia del Gabinetto del Ministero degli Affari Esteri, Rome 1890.
16. Historical statistics source, www.istat.it.
17. See I. Rosoni, *La Colonia Eritrea: La prima amministrazione coloniale italiana (1880-1912)*. op. cit., p. 103.
18. Ibid., p. 98.
19. N. Labanca, *Oltremare*. op. cit., p. 89.
20. Named after the geographical region of Mogadisco, and the location of the company's headquarters.
21. Law of December 31, 1899, No. 466, *Che approva la Convenzione relativa alla concessione, da parte del R. Governo, alla Società Anonima commerciale italiana del Benadir (Somalia italiana) delle città e dei territori del Benadir e del rispettivo "hinterland."* In *Gazzetta Ufficiale* No. 304 dd 31-12-1899.
22. See www.treccani.it.
23. Law of December 31, 1899, No. 466, art. 1.
24. Law of December 31, 1899, No. 466, art. 2.
25. Silver currency used in the 18th and 19th centuries for international trade, including Africa. In 1890, Italy began minting it with the image of Italian sovereigns for use in the Eritrean colony. It was replaced in 1936 by the Italian East African lira.
26. Law of December 31, 1899, No. 466, art. 4.
27. See A. Naletto, *Italiani in Somalia: Storia di un colonialismo straccione*. Cierre Edizioni, Caselle (VR) 2011.

28. N. Labanca, *Oltremare*. op. cit., p. 90.
29. G. Chiesi, E. Travelli, *Le questioni del Benadir, Atti e relazioni dei commissari della Società*. Tipografia Bellini, Milan 1904.
30. Royal Decree of January 26, 1905, No. 90, *Autorizzazione al procuratore del Re in Asmara di delegare funzionari per gli atti di istruttoria da compiersi nei possedimenti del Benadir*. In *Gazzetta Ufficiale* No. 77 01-04-1905.
31. Law of April 5, 1908, No. 161, *Per l'ordinamento della Somalia italiana*. In *Gazzetta Ufficiale* No. 102 30-04-1908.
32. See R. Rainero, *L'anticolonialismo italiano da Assab ad Adua*. op. cit.
33. For the history of the Italian concession in China, see A. Di Meo, *Tientsin: Storia delle relazioni tra Italia e Cina (1866-1947)*. Ginevra Bentivoglio Editoria, Rome 2015.
34 For an overview of the Boxer movement and its impact on the international relations of the Chinese Empire, see R. Bickers, R.G. Tiedemann (ed.), *The Boxers, China and the World*. Rowman & Littlefield Publishers, Lanham, Maryland 2007.
35. *Unequal treaties* refers to a series of agreements between the European powers and the monarchies of China, Korea and Japan during the 19th century, whereby the Asian countries were forced by the white imperialists to submit to humiliating trade conditions. For the case of China, see O. Coco, *Colonialismo europeo in Estremo Oriente: L'esperienza delle concessioni territoriali in Cina*. Edizioni Nuova Italia, Rome 2017, pp. 63-146.
36. The Boer Wars refers to two conflicts (1880-1881 and 1899-1902) that pitted Britain against the states formed by white settlers for control of South Africa.
37. "Gli avvenimenti della Cina: Chiese e case d'europei incendiate. Massacri di stranieri," in *Corriere della Sera*, June 17, 1900.
38. For the complete text and its media impact, see T. Klein, *Die Hunnenrede (1900)*, in J. Zimmerer, *Kein Platz an der Sonne: Erinnerungsorte der Deutsche Kolonialgeschichte*. Campus Verlag, Frankfurt am Main 2013, pp. 164-76.
39. "I fratelli Fazzari offrono i loro figli al Re per combattere in Cina," in *Corriere della Sera*, July 21, 1900.
40. Emilio Salgari, *Il sotterraneo della morte*. Newton Compton, Rome 1995 (first edition 1901).
41. See M. Lenci, *Corsari: Guerra, schiavi, rinnegati nel Mediterraneo*. Carocci, Rome 2006
42. G. Marilotti, *L'Italia e il Nord Africa: Storia dell'emigrazione sarda in Tunisia (1848-1914)*. Carocci, Rome 2006, p. 107.
43. "L'affare di Tunisi," in *Corriere della Sera*, April 6, 1881.

44. See L. Saiu, *La politica estera italiana dall'Unità a oggi*. op. cit., pp. 39-68.
45. The "Moroccan Crises" were a series of confrontations among the Western powers, namely Great Britain, France, Spain, and Germany, for control of Morocco. The Agadir Crisis in 1911 brought Franco-English and German colonial interests in direct conflict. See E. J. Hobsbawm, *The Age of Empires*. op. cit., pp. 321-22.
46. For a general overview of the upheavals in European politics in the first decade of the 20th century, see. C. Clark, *I sonnambuli: Come l'Europa arrivò alla Grande Guerra*. Laterza, Rome-Bari 2014.
47. See L. D'Angelo, *Pacifismo e umanità: Il pacifismo democratico italiano dalla guerra di Libia alla nascita della Società delle Nazioni*. il Mulino, Bologna 2016.
48. R. De Felice, *Mussolini il rivoluzionario (1883-1920)*. Einaudi, Turin 2018, p. 108.
49. "Verso la follia Tripolina, il proletariato contro la guerra," in *Avanti!*, September 25, 1911.
50. A. Schiavulli (ed.), *La guerra lirica. Il dibattito dei letterati italiani sull'impresa di Libia (1911-1912)*. Pozzi, Ravenna 2009, pp. 43 and ff.
51. Historian Nicola Labanca makes the case, beginning with the title, in one of his writings, *La guerra italiana per la Libia 1911-1931*. il Mulino, Bologna 2012.
52. Royal Decree of November 5, 1911, No. 1247, *Che pone sotto la sovranità piena ed intera del regno d'Italia la Tripolitania e la Cirenaica*. In *Gazzetta Ufficiale* 27-11-1911. The decree formally came into force on December 12 of the same year. The photo on the book's cover, of Italian troops in Libya, was taken on November 5, 1911.
53. N. Labanca, *Oltremare*. op. cit., p. 115.
54. A. Torre, "Le notizie false propalate all'estero sulla guerra in Tripolitania, il fatto inatteso e incompreso," in *Corriere della Sera*, November 2, 1911.
55. Ibid.
56. For an overview of Italian military operations in Libya, see. N. Labanca, *La guerra italiana per la Libia, 1911-1931*. op. cit.
57. For an account of the harshness of Italian concentration camps in Libya, see. A. Badr, *La resistenza libica all'occupazione italiana: Voci dal campo di El Agheila*. Clavilux Edizioni, Moretta 2019. Regarding the internment of Libyans in Italy, see. C.S. Capogreco, *I campi del duce: L'internamento civile nell'Italia fascista*. Einaudi, Turin 2004.
58. For example, A.A. Ahmida, *The Genocide in Libya: Shar, a Hidden Colonial History*. Routledge, London 2020. On the possible definition of Italian operations in Libya as "genocide," see M. Flores, *Il genocidio*. il Mulino, Bologna 2021, pp. 111-15.

59. Graziani would write a series of books applauding and justifying his actions in Libya, for example, *Pace Romana in Libia*. Mondadori, Milan 1937.

60. In Greek, literally, "twelve islands," namely, Astypalaia, Rhodes, Chalki, Karpathos, Kasos, Tilos, Nisyros, Kalymnos, Leros, Patmos, Symi, and Kos.

61. Source, www.seriestoriche.istat.it.

62. The Venizelos-Tittoni Agreement, signed in July 1919, took its name from the Greek prime minister and the Italian foreign minister.

63. F. Dessy, "Agricoltura nel Possedimento Italiano delle Isole Egee," in *Società Agraria di Bologna* (ed.), *La Valorizzazione Agraria delle Colonie Italiane*. Cappelli, Bologna 1933, pp. 230-31.

64 On the subject of citizenship for the inhabitants of the Dodecanese, see F. Espinosa, "Una cittadinanza imperiale basata sul consenso: il caso delle isole italiane dell'Egeo (1924-1940)," in S. Lorenzini and S.A. Bellezza (eds.), *Sudditi o cittadini? L'evoluzione delle appartenenze imperiali nella prima guerra Mondiale*. Viella, Rome 2018, pp. 189-204.

65. Ibid., p. 192.

66. E Transcript of the recording of Mussolini's speech proclaiming the Empire, May 9, 1936; see *Il fascismo in Italia: i discorsi 1935-1936*. Casa discografica Signal, 1972.

67. Even after the fall of Addis Ababa and the declaration of the end of hostilities, control over the vast Ethiopian Empire was quite limited. Some scholars argue that there was no actual peace for the entire duration of the occupation, among them Nicola Labanca, in his *La guerra d'Etiopia (1935-1941)*. il Mulino, Bologna 2015.

68. ⁶For a glimpse of the propaganda techniques employed by the Fascists to prepare Italians for the invasion of Ethiopia, see. M. Palmieri, *L'ora solenne: Gli italiani e la guerra d'Etiopia*. Baldini and Castoldi, Milan 2015.

69. On the propaganda accompanying the invasion of Ethiopia, see. N. Labanca, *Una guerra per l'impero: Memorie della campagna d'Etiopia*. il Mulino, Bologna 2005.

70. In his speech of June 10, 1940, Benito Mussolini asserted that what is about to begin "is a struggle between the impoverished masses with many strong arms and the creators of starvation who fiercely hold on to their monopoly over all the riches and all the gold of the earth; it is the struggle of fertile and youthful peoples against fading and sterile people; it is the struggle between two centuries and two ideologies." Cited in R. De Felice, *Mussolini il duce. II: Lo stato totalitario*. Einaudi, Turin 2019, p. 842.

71. At the beginning of the invasion, when news arrived of Italian troops entering the city of Adua, newspapers reported that the city had been "handed over" to Italian arms (*Corriere della Sera*, October 7, 1935).
72. N. Labanca, *Oltremare*. op. cit., 184.
73. A. Del Boca, *Gli italiani in Africa Orientale, III: la caduta dell'impero*. Mondadori, Milan 1992, pp. 237 and ff.
74. See (among many) R. De Felice, *Gli anni del consenso (1929-1936)*. Einaudi, Turin 2018, p. 637.
75. See G. Rochat, *Le guerre degli italiani (1935-1943)*. Einaudi, Turin 2005.

3. Contacts: Prejudices from Overseas

1. *La Cultura: Rivista Critica diretta dall'on. Bonghi*. M. Pasini Editore, Rome 1892, p. 155.
2. See *Gazzetta Ufficiale* No. 160 dd 10-07-1882, attachment.
3. The dual date disappeared from the deeds as soon as the Italian government—which did not consider a multicultural approach necessary—took control of the territory.
4. A "misappropriation" according to local law, but also according to Italian law, if it had been actually applied.
5. C.M. Cipolla, *Vele e cannoni*. il Mulino, Bologna 2011, p. 115. (First Italian edition 1983; first English edition 1965). On this subject, see also, J. Diamond, *Armi, acciaio e malattie: Breve storia del mondo negli ultimi tredicimila anni*. Einaudi, Turin 2006 (first edition 1998).
6. For example, with Royal Decree No. 3036 of December 20, 1923, *Modificazioni dell'ordinamento giudiziario della Somalia italiana*. In *Gazzetta Ufficiale* No. 21 25-01-1924—pertaining to matters of colonial justice—the administration of justice, previously in the hands of local representatives, was now centralized in the hands of Italian officials.
7. Above all, through the work of Cesare Maria De Vecchi, a high-ranking Fascist and a member of the quadrumvirate who, once he was appointed governor of Somalia, undertook a forced "pacification" through the destruction of the power balance established by local representatives (see entry "De Vecchi, Cesare Maria" in V. De Grazia and S. Luzzatto (eds.), in *Dizionario del Fascismo*. Einaudi, Turin 2019, pp. 425-28).
8. "La carovana abissina per Archiko," in *Corriere della Sera*, October 29, 1888.
9. See www.esercito.difesa.it/comunicazione.
10. See M. Sabattini, P. Santangelo, *Storia della Cina*. Laterza, Rome-Bari 2005.
11. The words of Tsar Nicholas I of Russia, describing the country in a conversation with the British ambassador in 1853. (See. R. Evans, *Alla conquista del potere: Europa 1815-1914*. Laterza, Rome-Bari 2020).

12. In Amharic, the language of the Ethiopian court, it literally means "Power of the Trinity." It is the ceremonial name assumed by Ras Tafari Makonnen, cousin of Emperor Menelik II, when he ascended to the throne in 1930.

13. "I Dankali per l'Esposizione di Torino," in *Corriere della Sera*, June 29, 1884.

14. For the dissemination of racist stereotypes in the late 19th century press, see M. Nani, *Ai confini della Nazione: Stampa e razzismo nell'Italia di fine Ottocento*. Carocci, Rome 2006.

15. For a history of the exhibiting of humans in Italy, see G. Abbattista, *Umanità in mostra: Esposizioni etniche e invenzioni esotiche in Italia (1880-1940)*. Edizioni Università di Trieste, Trieste 2013.

16. An idea widely circulated in the literature of the time. See P. Carmagnani, *Luoghi di tenebra: Lo spazio coloniale e il Romanzo*. Aracne, Rome 2011.

17. See the fact sheet of the Italian General Exhibition of 1884, in www.museotorino.it.

18. The exhibition program lists their names, religion, profession and origin: Haggi Ramadan and Mohammend Faragg, Muslims from Archico, near Massawa, goldsmiths; Alì Idris, Sudanese Muslim, also a goldsmith; Tafarì Gosciù, Coptic Christian from Adua, described as a "painter and designer of simple illustrated colour postcards"; Mohammed Ibié and Mohammed Abd-Haggi, both Muslims from Adua, an embroiderer and weaver, respectively; Idris Omer, a Muslim from Cheren, Eritrea, a saddler, maker of sandals and slippers; finally, the only woman, Alfiot Hamed, is described as old and a Muslim from Cassala in British Sudan, a weaver of plant fibres. Curiously enough, only three of the eight deportees are actually Italian colonial subjects. The others were randomly chosen to pose as Eritrean artisans. See *Le mostre coloniali all'esposizione internazionale di Torino del 1911, Relazione generale*. Tipografia Nazionale Berterio, Rome 1913.

19. For an overview of "Italian colonial literature," see (among others) G. Tomasello, *L'Africa tra mito e realtà: Storia della letteratura coloniale italiana*. Sellerio, Palermo 2004.

20. V. Mantegazza, *Da Massaua a Saati: Narrazione della spedizione italiana del 1888 in Abissinia*. Fratelli Treves, Milan 1888, pp. 23-24.

21. P. Mantegazza, "Prime linee di fisiognomia comparata delle razze umane. Lesioni artificiali del corpo umano: Tatuaggio e pitture." In *Gazzetta medica italiana*. Lombardia, Giuseppe Chiusi Editore, Milan 1862, pp. 379-80.

22. A. Scarsella, "Note su fumetto e imitazione storica. Parodia, allegoria, memoria," in N. Spagnolli, C. Gallo, G. Bonomi (eds.); *Il Fumetto: fonte e interprete della Storia*. Betelgeuse Editore, Rovereto 2015, p. 71.

23. "L'entusiasmo degli ascari per l'Italia," *Corriere della Sera*, July 29, 1912.

24. Semi-monthly magazine printed from August 5, 1938 to June 20, 1943. It featured pseudo-scientific articles on racism, anti-Semitism and Fascist imperialism. It quickly became the "megaphone" of Italian racism. See V. Pisanty, *La Difesa della razza: Antologia 1938-1943*. Bompiani, Milan 2019.

25. G. Landra, "Razza e lavoro," in *Difesa della razza*, II, 12: 44-45 (April 20, 1939), quoted in V. Pisanty, *La Difesa della razza*. op.cit., p. 168.

26. https://patrimonio.archivioluce.com/luce-web/detail/IL5000061569/2/gondar-antica-capitale-etiopica.html?startPage=0.

27. F. Hellwald, G. Strafforello, *Africa, secondo le notizie più recenti*. Loescher, Florence-Rome 1885, p. 477.

28. See L. Robecchi Bricchetti, *Somalia e Benadir, viaggio di esplorazione nell'Africa orientale: Prima traversata della Somalia, compiuta per incarico della Società geografica italiana*. Aliprandi, Milan 1899.

29. See www.treccani.it.

30. Royal Decree of December 3, 1934, No. 2012, *Ordinamento organico per l'amministrazione della Libia*, in *Gazzetta Ufficiale* 21-12-1934.

31. See www.treccani.it.

32. In the collective memory of Italians, the "Abyssinian War "most often recalls the Italian-Ethiopian conflict of 1895-96 that culminated in the defeat at Adua. Among some historians, a distinction is made between the First Italo-Abyssinian War (1895-96) and the Second Italo-Abyssinian War (1935-36). See A. Del Boca, *Italiani, brava gente?* op. cit., pp. 17 and ff.

33. Symbol of the Hebrew tribe of Judah, it was adopted as the emblem of the Ethiopian monarch and then of the Empire itself to recall the legend that the Ethiopian monarchy is descended from King Solomon and the Queen of Sheba.

34. Royal Decree of July 1, 1936, No. 1019, *Ordinamento e amministrazione dell'Africa Orientale Italiana*. In *Gazzetta Ufficiale* 136 13-06-1936.

35. Ibid., art. 1.

36. See S. Bellucci, *Storia delle guerre africane: Dalla fine del colonialismo al neoliberismo globale*. Carocci, Rome 2006.

37. On the ambiguous construction of the concept of nationhood in Italy, let me quote my book, *Prima gli Italiani! (Sì, ma quali?)*. Laterza, Rome-Bari 2021.

38. It was originally created as *Club Africano* in 1880.

39. See B. Droz, *Storia della decolonizzazione nel XX secolo*. Bruno Mondadori, Milan 2007 and D.K. Kennedy, *Storia della Decolonizzazione*. il Mulino, Bologna 2017.

40. G. Stefani, *Colonia per maschi, Italiani in Africa orientale: una storia di genere*. Ombre Corte, Verona 2007.

41. For the relationship between the women's movement in Italy and the colonial question, see C. Papa, *Sotto altri cieli: L'oltremare nel movimento femminile italiano*. Viella, Rome 2011.

42. See *I censimenti nell'Italia unita: Le fonti di stato della popolazione tra XIX e XXI secolo*. Atti del Convegno "I censimenti fra passato, presente e future." Turin, December 4-6, 2010, "Annali di statistica," Anno 141, Serie XII, Vol. 2, p. 263.

43. See entry "Africa Orientale Italiana," in www.treccani.it.

44. See *I censimenti nell'Italia unita*. op. cit., p. 269.

45. F. Manetta, *La razza negra nel suo stato selvaggio in Africa e nella sua duplice condizione di emancipata e di schiava in America*. Tipografia del commercio, Turin 1864.

46. *Geografia per tutti*. Vallardi Editore, Anno V, No. 1, January 15, 1895, p. 53.

47. "Viaggio nella colonia primigenia: le belle donne di Assab," in *La Stampa*. December 28, 1930

48. G. Piccinini, *Guerra d'Africa*. Edoardo Perino Editore, Rome 1887.

49. Ibid., vol. I, pp. 3-4.

50. Ibid., vol. I, p. 13.

51. G.B. Licata, *Assab e i Danàchili*. Treves, Milan 1885.

52. On the creation of the image of women in the colonial context, both white and black, also see M. di Barbora, "Colonialismo e identità nazionale di genere tra fascismo ed età repubblicana," in V. Deplano, A. Pes (eds.), *Quel che resta dell'impero*. op. cit., pp. 191-208.

53. "Bellezze negre a Mogadiscio," in *La Stampa*. May 31, 1934.

54. https://patrimonio.archivioluce.com/luce-web/detail/IL5000022679/2/documentario-sulla-regione-della-dancalia.html?startPage=0.

55. E. Ertola, *In terra d'Africa: Gli italiani che colonizzarono l'impero*. Laterza, Rome-Bari 2017, p. 159.

56. F. Liperi, *Storia della canzone italiana*. RAI-ERI, Rome 1999, p. 48.

57. S. Pivato, *La storia leggera: Uso pubblico della storia nella canzone italiana*. il Mulino, Bologna 2002, pp. 65 and ff.

58. F. Liperi, *Storia della canzone italiana*. op. cit., p. 123.

59. See I. Scego, "La vera storia di 'Faccetta Nera,'" in *Internazionale*. August 6, 2015.

60. See L. Gangale, *La donna che osò tenere testa a Indro Montanelli*, www.glistatigenerali.com, June 21, 2020.

61. See R. Bonavita, *Spettri dell'altro: Letteratura e razzismo nell'Italia contemporanea*. il Mulino, Bologna 2009.

62. E. Flaiano, *Tempo di uccidere*. Adelphi, Milan 2020 (first edition 1947).
63. For an analysis of Flaiano's novel from a postcolonial perspective, see B. Tonzar, *Colonie letterarie: Immagini dell'Africa italiana dalla fine del sogno mperiale agli anni sessanta*. Carocci, Rome 2017, pp. 55-100.
64. See. G. Stefani, *Colonia per maschi*. op. cit., p. 165.
65. Pseudonym of the dancer Kiash Nanah (1936-2014).
66. Possibly an Islamic prayer rug. See "Nove persone a giudizio per lo scandalo del 'Rugantino.'" In *Corriere della Sera*. April 9, 1960.

4. Returns: Colonial Memory and Colonial Oblivion

1. Giarabub is an oasis on the border between Libya and Egypt, the scene of several clashes between Italian and British troops, from December 1940 to March 1941 in which the British prevailed.
2. I. Montanelli, *XX Battaglione eritreo*. Rizzoli, Milan 2010 (first edition 1936).
3. Ibid., p. 1.
4. For a broader examination of the evolution of recollections about the war in Ethiopia, see N. Labanca, *Una guerra per l'impero: Memorie della campagna d'Etiopia*. il Mulino, Bologna 2005.
5. On the legal and social difficulties experienced by the children born of these unions following the end of colonialism, see V. Deplano, *La madrepatria è una terra straniera: Libici eritrei e somali nell'Italia del dopoguerra (1945-1960)*. Le Monnier, Florence 2017.
6. On career opportunities available in the civil service under the colonial system, see C. Giorgi, *L'Africa come carriera: Funzioni e funzionari del colonialismo italiano*. Carocci, Rome 2012.
7. See seriestoriche.istat.it.
8. G. P. Calchi Novati, *L'Africa d'Italia*. op. cit., p. 199.
9. See www.seriestoriche.istat.it.
10. Law of May 24, 1903, No. 205, *Ordinamento della colonia Eritrea*. In *Gazzetta Ufficiale* 130 04-06-1903.
11. The term "non-indigenous" includes all whites people in the colony—Italians and foreigners alike—differentiated from the rest of the population by ethnicity and not by citizenship.
12. S. Palma, "L'oro e la scrittura: La formazione della gioventù eritrea nelle scuole elementari dei primi anni trenta," in AA. VV., *Colonia e postcolonia come spazi diasporici: Attraversamenti di memorie, identità e confini nel Corno d'Africa*. Carocci, Rome 2011, p. 138.
13. S. Palma, "Educare alla subalternità: Prassi e politiche scolastiche nella colonia eritrea," in B.M. Carcangiu, T. Negash (eds.), *L'Africa orientale italiana nel dibattito contemporaneo*. Carocci, Rome 2007, p. 234.

14. For how Libyans were perceived by Italians during the colonial period, see G. Bassi, *Sudditi di Libia*. Mimesis, Sesto San Giovanni 2018.
15. Royal Decree of June 1, 1919, No. 931, *Che approva le norme fondamentali per l'assetto della Tripolitania*. In *Gazzetta Ufficiale* 145 19-06-1919.
16. Royal Decree of October 31, 1919, No. 2401, *Che approva le norme fondamentali per l'assetto della Cirenaica*. In *Gazzetta Ufficiale* 302 23-12-1919.
17. Law of June 26 1927, No. 1013, *Legge organica per l'amministrazione della Tripolitania e della Cirenaica*. In *Gazzetta Ufficiale* 148 28-06-1927.
18. As specified in Articles 29 and 30 of the Law: Art. 29. The following are Italian-Libyan citizens: children, wherever born, of a father who is an Italian-Libyan citizen or, if the latter is unknown, of a mother who is an Italian-Libyan citizen; a woman married to an Italian-Libyan citizen; those born in Tripolitania or Cyrenaica, wherever they reside, who are not citizens of Metropolitan Italy or foreign citizens or subjects according to Italian law; children of born unknown persons found in Tripolitania or Cyrenaica are presumed to have been born there until proven otherwise. Art. 30. All persons, who reside in Tripolitania or Cyrenaica, and who are not citizens of Metropolitan Italy or foreign citizens or subjects, are presumed to be Libyan-Italian citizens.
19 See F. Renucci, "La strumentalizzazione del concetto di cittadinanza in Libia negli anni trenta," in *Quaderni fiorentini per la storia del pensiero giuridico moderno*. 2005, No. 33-34, pp. 319-42.
20. Royal Decree of January 9, 1939, No. 70, *Aggregazione delle quattro provincie libiche al territorio del Regno d'Italia e concessione ai libici musulmani di una cittadinanza italiana speciale con statuto personale e successorio musulmano*. In *Gazzetta Ufficiale* No. 28 03-02-1939.
21. For the effect of Fascist propaganda on the perceptions of colonists and Italians in general, see essays by G. Mancosu, M. Piras, and M.A. Nughedu in A. Pes (eds.), *Mare Nostrum: Il colonialismo fascista tra realtà e rappresentazione*. AIPSA Edizioni, Cagliari 2012.
22. See A. Urbano, A. Varsori, *Mogadiscio 1948: Un eccidio di italiani tra decolonizzazione e Guerra Fredda*. il Mulino, Bologna 2019.
23. M.A. Nughedu, "La Libia: un esempio del colonialismo italiano," in A. Pes (ed.), *Mare Nostrum. Il colonialismo fascista tra realtà e rappresentazione*. op. cit., pp. 240-41.
24. Source: AA.VV., *I censimenti nell'Italia unita*. op. cit., p. 269.
25. M.A. Nughedu, *La Libia*. op. cit., p. 250.

26. https://patrimonio.archivioluce.com/luce-web/detail/IL5000094757/ 2/unraro-documento-cinematografico-sulla-colonizzazione-ital-iana-libia.html?

27. A.M. Morone, *L'ultima colonia: Come l'Italia è tornata in Africa (1950- 1960)*. Laterza, Rome-Bari 2011, p. 41.

28. See G. Mosse, *La nazionalizzazione delle masse: Simbolismo politico e movimenti di massa in Germania (1815-1933)*. il Mulino, Bologna 2009 (first edition 1975).

29. The full text of the treaty is kept, among other places, in the Digital Archive of the Chamber of Deputies, www.archivio.camera.it.

30. C. Sforza, *Cinque anni a Palazzo Chigi: La politica estera italiana dal 1947 al 1951*. Atlante, Rome 1952, p. 13.

31. N. Srivastava, *Italian Colonialism and Resistances to Empire (1930-1970)*. Palgrave Macmillan, London 2018, pp. 195 and ff.

32. Acts of Parliament, Chambre, *Discussione del 4 febbraio 1950*. In www.archivio.camera.it.

33. See FAO 2019, *Dentro la FAO-Storia di un forum globale*. Rome 2019.

34. On this subject, see my volume, *Ma perché siamo ancora fascisti? Un conto rimasto aperto*. Bollati Boringhieri, Turin 2020.

35. A. Ungari, "I monarchici italiani e la questione coloniale (1947-1952)," in V. Deplano, A. Pes (eds), *Quel che resta dell'impero*. op. cit., p. 401.

36. G.P. Calchi Novati, *Il canale della Discordia; Suez e la politica estera italiana*. Quattro Venti, Urbino 1998.

37. For the true strength of the local resistance movement in Ethiopia, see N. Srivastava, *Italian Colonialism and Resistances to Empire (1930-1970)*. Palgrave Macmillan, London 2018.

38. See F. Focardi, *Il cattivo tedesco e il bravo italiano: La rimozione delle colpe della seconda guerra mondiale*. Laterza, Rome-Bari 2014.

39. See I. Campbell, *Il massacro di Addis Abeba: Una vergogna italiana*. Rizzoli, Milano 2018, and P. Borruso, *Debre Libanos 1937; Il più grave crimine di guerra dell'Italia*. Laterza, Rome-Bari 2020.

40. See S. Belladonna, *Gas in Etiopia: I Crimini rimossi dell'Italia coloniale*. Neri Pozza, Vicenza 2015.

41. On the (neglected) politics of memory relating to Italian crimes, also see A. Stramaccioni, *Crimini di Guerra: Storia e memoria del caso italiano*. Laterza, Rome-Bari 2018.

42. G. Mondaini, *Manuale di storia e legislazione coloniale del Regno d'Italia*. Sampaolesi, Rome 1927.

43. R. Ciasca, *Storia coloniale dell'Italia contemporanea: Da Assab all'im-peroI*. Hoepli, Milano 1938.

44. J. L. Miège, *L'imperialismo coloniale italiano dal 1870 ai giorni nostri*. Rizzoli, Milan 1976 (1968 edition and original French edition).

45. N. Labanca, *Oltremare*. op. cit., p. 9.
46. He is the author, in 1938, of the already cited, *Storia coloniale dell'Italia contemporanea*; elected senator from 1948 to 1950; as a member of the Committee on Foreign Affairs and the Colonies, he actively participated in discussions on re-arranging relations between Italy and its former colonies (see www.senato.it).
47. G.P. Calchi Novati, *L'Africa d'Italia*. op. cit., p. 41.
48. G. Rochat, "Colonialismo," in N. Tranfaglia (ed.), *Il Mondo contemporaneo: Storia d'Italia*. La Nuova Italia, Florence 1978, Vol. 1, p. 109.
49. A.M. Morone, "I custodi della memoria: Il Comitato per la documentazione dell'opera dell'Italia in Africa," in *Zapruder: Rivista di storia della conflittualità sociale*, September-December 2019, pp. 24-38.
50. G.P. Calchi Novati, *L'Africa d'Italia*. op. cit., p. 42.
51. S. Palma, "Il colonialismo italiano tra riabilitazioni e rimozioni," September 20, 2019, www.ispionline.it.
52. On Italian film crews engaged in Fascist propaganda regarding Africa, see G. Mancosu, "L'impero visto da una cinepresa: Il reparto foto-cinematografico 'Africa Orientale' dell'Istituto Luce," in V. Deplano, A. Pes (ed.), *Quel che resta dell'impero*. op. cit., pp. 259-78.
53. See *Gli Annali dell'Africa Italiana: le opere pubbliche*. Mondadori, Milan 1939.
54. E. Ertola, "Predatori fascisti dell'Impero," in P. Giovannini e M. Palla (eds.), *Il fascismo dalle mani sporche*. Laterza, Rome-Bari 2019, pp. 218-35.
55. Cited by G.L. Podestà, "Le città dell'Impero: La fondazione di una nuova civiltà italiana in Africa orientale," in *Città e Storia, Vol. IV, No. 1*. Rome 2009, p. 133.
56. Giuseppe Cobolli Gigli (1892-1987), Minister of Public Works from 1935 to 1939.
57. Cited in E. Ertola, *In terra d'Africa*. op. cit., p. 36.
58. See G. Rochat, *Italo Balbo*. UTET, Turin 1986, pp. 265-66.
59. See my volume, *Mussolini Also Did a Lot of Good, The Spread of Historical Amnesia*, Baraka Books, Montréal, 2021.
60. See V. Deplano, *La madrepatria è una terra straniera*. op. cit.
61. Ibid., p. 107.
62. About 2000 people, ibid., p. 108. This figure may seem small, given that the "meticcio" population in Eritrea at the time was about 15,000. But the number must be assessed on the assumption that the vast majority of this segment of the population could not apply for Italian citizenship (e.g. the unrecognized children of mixed unions).
63. A.M. Morone, *L'ultima colonia*. op. cit., p. 58.

64. A. Del Boca, *Italiani, brava gente?* op. cit., p. 248.
65. With the Royal Decree of April 8, 1937, No. 431 (*Gazzetta Ufficiale* 88 15-04-1937), the old Ministry of the Colonies, established in 1912, took the new name of Ministry of Italian Africa, aligning it linguistically with the regime's propaganda narrative.
66. M. Morone, *L'ultima colonia.* op. cit., p. 175.

5. Regurgitations: What's Left?

1. On the creation and composition of Libyan, Eritrean, Somali, and Ethiopian communities in Italy, see V. Deplano, *La madrepatria è una terra straniera.* op. cit., pp. 23-85.
2. N. Zingarelli, *Vocabolario della Lingua Italiana*, Zanichelli, Bologna 2002.
3. Reported in www.dizionario.internazionale.it/parola/ambaradan.
4. A. Del Boca, *Italiani brava gente?* op. cit., p. 192.
5. S. Vazzana, "'Ambaradan,' quando una parola nasce da un genocidio," *La Stampa.* February 15, 2017.
6. For all, see F. Melandri, *Sangue giusto.* Rizzoli, Milan 2017 and Wu Ming I, R. Santachiara, *Point Lenana.* Einaudi, Turin 2013.
7. R. Cappelli, "Raggi: la fermata Amba Aradam della Metro C sarà intitolata a Giorgio Marincola," in *La Repubblica.* August 1, 2020.
8. For Rome, as a unique example of an ongoing street-naming battle, see R. Bianchi, I. Scego, N. Terranova, A. Branchi, *Roma negata: Percorsi postcoloniali nella città.* Ediesse, Rome 2014.
9. "Dal tucùl al grattacielo," in *Corriere della Sera.* August 8, 1969.
10. For an overview, see https://www.youtube.com/results?search_query=il+pianto+di+zambo.
11. *I due nemici* (Italy, 1961).
12. *El Alamein* (Italy, 2002).
13. *Nassiriya: Per non dimenticare* (Italy, 2007).
14. *Le rose del deserto* (Italy, 2006).
15. *Riusciranno i nostri eroi a ritrovare l'amico misteriosamente scomparso in Africa?* (Italy, 1968).
16. *Io sto con gli ippopotami* (Italy, 1979).
17. See T. Petrovich Njiegosh, A. Scacchi, *Parlare di razza: La lingua del colore tra Italia e Stati Uniti.* Ombre Corte, Verona 2012.
18. P. Dogliani, *Il fascismo degli Italiani: una storia sociale.* UTET, Turin 2008, p. 257.
19. Running barefoot was a last-minute decision, resulting from the fact that the shoes provided by the sponsors hurt. Bikila had used shoes during training and would continue to do so throughout his career. For the story and the myth that arose around that marathon, see S.

Coher, *Vincere a Roma: L'indimenticabile impresa di Abebe Bikila*, 66thand2nd, Rome 2020. Also see the feature film *L'alteta: Abebe Bikila*, Ethiopia-USA-Germany 2009.

20. *Guess Who's Coming to Dinner* (USA, 1967).
21. "Lo scrivo al giornale: un sussulto irrazionale," in *Corriere della Sera*. April 24, 1968.
22. On the continued relationship between racist stereotypes and dirtiness, see C. Lombardi-Diop, "Igiene, pulizia, bellezza e razza: La 'bianchezza' nella cultura italiana dal fascismo al dopoguerra." In T. Petrovich Njiegosh, A. Scacchi (eds.), *Parlare di razza*. op. cit., pp. 78-96.
23. Broadcast in the USA from 1972 to 1977, aired in Italy in the 1980s.
24. An interesting analysis of translation problems regarding US television series that feature black characters, showing the loss of nuance and the simplification of stereotypes to appeal to Italian viewers, can be found in L. Buonomo, "Indovina chi viene a cena? La rappresentazione degli afroamericani nel doppiaggio italiano di *The Jeffersons*," in T. Petrovich Njiegosh, A. Scacchi (eds.), *Parlare di razza*. op. cit., pp. 220-40.
25. *I ragazzi della 3a C* (Italy 1987-1989).
26. For the many instances of more or less explicit racism on Italian television, see O.Q.D. Obasuyi, *Corpi estranei: Il razzismo rimosso che appiattisce la diversità*. People, Gallarate 2020.
27. "Gheddafi con la foto provocazione, eroe anticoloniale sull'alta uniforme," in *Corriere della Sera*. June 10, 2009; M. Innocenti, "Chi è al-Mukhtar, l'uomo nella foto sul petto di Gheddafi," in *Il Sole 24 ore*. June 10, 2009; and "Sul petto di Gheddafi la foto del resistente in catene, 'Per noi è come una croce,'" in *La Stampa*. June 11, 2009.
28. The Senussi are a Sunni Islamic order that organized anti-Italian resistance in the region of Cyrenaica in the eastern part of present-day Libya. The Al-Sanusi royal family ruled over the United Kingdom of Libya from 1950 to 1969.
29. *Lion of the Desert*. (Asad al-ṣaḥrā', Libya, 1981).
30. A. Del Boca, "Chi ha paura di Omar?" *Il Messaggero*, March 14, 1983.
31. "Disappunto italiano per un film libico che accusa i nostri soldati," in ANSA, December 30, 1981.
32. "No al film su Graziani," in *La Repubblica*, March 8, 1987.
33. "Il leone del deserto torna a ruggire su Sky," in Sky TG24, June 11, 2009.
34 34 UNOSOM, "United Nations Operations in Somalia," was the name given to the first international operation in Somalia, starting in April 1992. It was replaced by UNITAF, starting in May 1993—when the

rules of engagement were changed due to an escalation in the fighting—and then by UNOSOM II, which lasted until March 1995.
35. See "missioni internazionali" in www.esercito.difesa.it.
36. A first-hand account of the Italian contingent's experiences as part of the UN mission in Lebanon is given by Franco Angioni, the army general in charge of operations, in *Un soldato italiano in Libano*, Rizzoli, Milan 1984.
37. For an analysis of the Italian military's new role in international missions, see F. Battistelli, *Soldati: sociologia dei militari italiani nell'era del peace-keeping*, Carocci, Rome 2001 (first edition 1996).
38. For example, most Italians don't know that bilateral agreements have been in place since 1960, allowing Somali students to study at Italian universities, and that a number of lectures at the University of Mogadishu are given in Italian by native speakers.
39. The Italian figures were reported by the Ministry of Defence, while the Somalis figures are estimates, due to the impossibility of conducting investigations in the field. Moreover, the estimates include the dead among the Somali police force, rebels, and the civilian population.
40. See B. Loi, *Peace-keeping, guerra o pace? Una risposta italiana: l'operazione Ibis in Somalia*. Vallecchi, Florence 2004.
41. F. Battistelli, *Soldati*. op. cit., p. 96.
42. See www.esercito.difesa.it.
43. For a reconstruction of the case, see www.ilariaalpi.it, *Il caso Ilaria Alpi*.
44. The excerpt of the interview given to *La Gazzetta del Mezzogiorno* on April 21, 1997 can be found in the proceedings of the Fourth Parliamentary Standing Committee on Defence (see *19° resoconto stenografico IV Commissione, seduta 19 giugno 1997*, p. 3).
45. *Epoca* and *Sette*, June 7, 1993 issues.
46. *19° resoconto stenografico IV Commissione*, session 19 June 1997, p. 9.
47. *Panorama*. June 26, 1997, p. 23.
48. *1° resoconto stenografico IV Commissione Permanente (Difesa)*, session 21 January 1998, p. 12.
49. For a description of the stele, see M. Santi, *La stele di Axum da bottino di guerra a patrimonio dell'umanità*, Mimesis, Rome 2014.
50. See www.archivio.camera.it.
51. Decree by the President of the Republic, June 15, 1956, No. 643, *Esecuzione dell'accordo tra l'Italia e l'Etiopia, con annessi e note, per il regolamento delle questioni economiche e finanziarie derivanti dal Trattato di pace, concluso in Addis Abeba il 5 marzo 1956*. In *Gazzetta Ufficiale* No. 172 12-7-1956.

52. "In cambio dell'obelisco di Axum si propone di costruire una Chiesa in Etiopia," in *Corriere della Sera*. March 8, 1956.

53. "I ventidue missini fermati a "In cambio dell'obelisco di Axum si propone di costruire una Chiesa in Etiopia," in *Corriere della Sera*. April 24, 1956.

54. "Scalfaro annuncia ad Addis Abeba la restituzione dell'obelisco di Axum," in *l'Unità*, November 25, 1997.

55. See www.esteri.it.

56. See "Etiopia: Sgarbi, la stele di Axum doveva rimanere a Roma," in *Adnkronos*. March 31, 2007.

57. www.whc.unesco.org/en/list/15/.

58. V. Sgarbi, "Amaro destino della stele di Axum," in *Il Giornale*. April 2, 2007.

Conclusion

1. www.jacobinitalia.it/la-storia-nascosta-dellanticolonialismo-italiano/.

MORE FROM BARAKA BOOKS

MUSSOLINI ALSO DID A LOT OF GOOD
The Spread of Historical Amnesia
Francesco Filippi

CANADA'S LONG FIGHT AGAINST DEMOCRACY
Yves Engler and Owen Schalk

ARSENIC MON AMOUR
Letters of Love and Rag
Jean-Lou David & Gabrielle Izaguirré-Falardeau
(Translated by Mary O'Connor)

THE SEVEN NATIONS OF CANADA 1660-1860
Solidarity, Vision and Independence in the
St. Lawrence Valley
Jean-Pierre Sawaya

THE LEGACY OF LOUIS RIEL
Leader of the Métis People
John Andrew Morrow

AFTER ALL WAS LOST
Resilience of a Rwandan Family Orphaned on Apr. 6 '94
When the Rwandan
President's Plane was Shot Down
Alice Nsabimana

ISRAEL: A BEACHHEAD IN THE MIDDLE EAST
From European Colony to US Power Projection Platform
Stephen Gowans

MIX
Paper
FSC® C100212

Printed by Imprimerie Gauvin
Gatineau, Québec